AF255536

PHILOSOPHY MADE CLEAR

Understanding David Hume

A Clear, Guided Journey Through His Philosophy as a Whole

by

Luis Arturo Pelayo

Trazo

2026

To Ale, Luciana, and Josemaría:

I wrote this book during time I should have
spent with you.

Thank you for being patient, for always believing
in me, and most importantly, for your love.
Without that, none of this would matter.

CONTENTS

PREFACE

The origin of this book goes back to the late 1990s, when I was an undergraduate student of philosophy at Intercontinental University in Mexico. Like many students newly arriving in the world of philosophy, I initially found classical metaphysics particularly difficult to grasp. I struggled to see the point of devoting countless hours to reflections on notions such as *being qua being*, the distinction between *essence* and *existence*, or the possibility that change might be an illusion. At that stage, none of this seemed to offer anything concrete for understanding everyday life.

Philosophy often appeared to me as a discipline trapped in endless abstract discussions—an intellectual pastime reserved for a privileged few, one that solved no real problems and did little to improve human or social conditions. I found myself asking what practical value there could be in speculating about universals, substances, or first causes when no empirical verification of such entities seemed possible.

Although I gradually became familiar with these concepts—since they form the point of departure of the philosophical tradition and help us understand how philosophical thought has developed over centuries—it was the thinkers of the Enlightenment who truly awakened my interest.

Skeptical of, and often openly hostile to, classical metaphysics, philosophers such as Voltaire, Diderot, and Hume regarded it as an intellectual burden: a form of speculation that, rather than clarifying reality, obscured it. They advocated a more empirical and experience-based approach to philosophy, convinced that knowledge should be grounded in observation, human nature, and practical reason rather than inherited metaphysical categories.

This confidence in experience, in reason applied to moral, social, and political life, and in a philosophy concerned with freedom and human progress rather than abstract speculation, resonated deeply with me as a young student. It is therefore hardly surprising that David Hume—central to the Enlightenment reaction against metaphysics and arguably the most radical empiricist of his time—captured my attention.

When, during my second year of undergraduate studies, I was required to choose a thinker on whom to write a comprehensive dissertation traditionally known as *Universa Philosophica*—a term that referred to philosophy understood as a unified whole rather than as a set of specialized disciplines—I did not hesitate to choose Hume. The seed of this book, as well as its overall structure, can be traced back to that formative moment, when I first attempted to present Hume's thought in a coherent and unified manner.

Although I would later come to recognize the limitations of his philosophy and, in some respects, come to think differently from him, my sustained engagement with Hume's work proved intellectually rewarding. It is from that experience that these pages emerged, written with a deliberately pedagogical and accessible purpose.

INTRODUCTION

Reading David Hume directly can be a challenging experience. His arguments are subtle, his conclusions often unsettling, and his philosophy is spread across multiple works that address different problems from different angles. For many readers, this results in a fragmented understanding: one may grasp Hume's skepticism about causality, for example, while remaining unclear about how this skepticism connects to his views on morality, religion, society, or human nature as a whole.

At the same time, many introductions to Hume presuppose a technical background that non-specialists do not possess, making the first encounter with his philosophy unnecessarily difficult.

This book seeks to respond to that difficulty. Its aim is not to present a technical or scholarly commentary on Hume's texts, but to offer a clear, guided, and reader-friendly journey through his philosophy as an integrated whole. Rather than treating Hume's ideas as isolated theses, this book presents them as parts of a coherent philosophical vision grounded in an empiricist understanding of human nature.

Accordingly, this book is intended for readers who wish to *understand* Hume rather than to specialize in him: readers without formal academic training in philosophy, students at an introductory level, autodidacts, and anyone interested in gaining a clear and structured overview of one of the most influential thinkers of modern philosophy. It is not a critical edition of Hume's works, nor a technical reconstruction of scholarly debates. Its purpose is orientation and comprehension, not academic specialization.

What distinguishes this introduction is its systematic scope and pedagogical continuity. The book follows Hume's philosophy across the major domains in which it unfolds: the problem of knowledge, the question of being, the philosophy of nature, the problem of God, moral philosophy, social philosophy, and philosophical anthropology. Throughout, the aim is to show how these areas are internally connected and how Hume's empiricist principles shape his answers to each of them. In this way, the reader is not presented with disconnected topics, but with a unified account of Hume's thought.

The book may be read from beginning to end as a continuous exposition, but it is also structured so that individual chapters can be approached independently by readers with specific interests. Each chapter builds on the previous ones conceptually, yet none requires specialized prior knowledge. The progression is designed to accompany the reader step by step, allowing Hume's philosophy to emerge gradually and coherently.

The exposition begins with Hume's theory of knowledge, since epistemology constitutes the foundation of his philosophical system and the starting point of modern philosophy more generally. From there, we proceed to ontology, the philosophy of nature, the problem of God, moral philosophy, social philosophy, and finally an analysis of the human being. This order reflects Hume's own method: the consistent application of his empiricist principles to all areas of inquiry.

In developing these themes, this book draws primarily on *A Treatise of Human Nature*, where Hume elaborates his most systematic account of knowledge, nature, and the self. The *Enquiry Concerning Human Understanding* and the *Enquiry Concerning the Principles of Morals* are used to refine and clarify key aspects of his epistemology and ethics, while texts such as the *Dissertation on the Passions*, the *Political Essays*, the *Dialogues Concerning Natural Religion*, and *The Natural History of Religion* provide essential material for understanding his views on human nature, society, and religion.

Hume emerges from this exposition not as a distant historical figure, but as a philosopher whose questions remain deeply relevant. His reflections on the limits of reason, the foundations of morality, the role of passion in human action, and the nature of social life continue to illuminate contemporary debates.

By presenting his philosophy in a clear and unified manner, this book aims to help the reader engage with Hume not as a relic of the past, but as a living interlocutor whose thought still challenges and informs our understanding of ourselves and the world.

BIOGRAPHICAL NOTE

David Hume was born in Edinburgh, Scotland, in 1711. Although he initially studied law at the university of his native city—largely under the influence of his family—his interests soon turned toward literature, history, and philosophy. From an early age, Hume was dissatisfied with the abstract and speculative character that philosophy often assumed, and he became convinced that a radical change in approach was necessary if philosophy was to contribute meaningfully to human understanding.

After an unsuccessful attempt to establish himself in business in Bristol, Hume decided, at the age of eighteen, to devote himself entirely to intellectual pursuits. This decision led him to France, where he spent several formative years in Reims and later in La Flèche (1734–1737). It was during this period that he composed *A Treatise of Human Nature*, the work in which he first articulated his ambitious philosophical project: to apply an experimental, experience-based method to the study of human nature.

Published in 1739–1740, the *Treatise* initially attracted little attention and, in Hume's own words, "fell dead-born from the press." Undeterred, Hume later reworked key parts of the book in a more accessible form, publishing them as *An Enquiry Concerning Human Understanding* (1751) and *An Enquiry Concerning the Principles of Morals* (1751–1752). Although these works did not immediately bring him the recognition he desired, they would later come to be regarded as central texts of modern philosophy.

Hume's intellectual career unfolded within the broader context of the Enlightenment, a period marked by profound transformations in science, politics, and society. Modern philosophy had shifted its focus away from medieval metaphysics and religious authority toward reason, experience, and the study of human nature. Advances in the natural sciences—particularly the influence of Isaac Newton—reinforced the conviction that knowledge should be grounded in observation and that philosophical inquiry should remain within the limits of experience.[1]

Against this backdrop, Hume developed one of the most consistent and far-reaching forms of empiricism. He questioned the possibility of knowledge beyond perception, challenged traditional notions of substance and causality, and argued that reason alone is incapable of motivating human action. In ethics, he grounded moral judgments in sentiment and utility rather than in divine command or rational deduction.

In the philosophy of religion, he subjected arguments for the existence of God and religious belief to skeptical scrutiny, while in social and political thought he emphasized convention, utility, and the social nature of human beings.

Despite early controversies and professional setbacks, Hume eventually achieved widespread recognition. His *Political Discourses* (1752) and, later, his multivolume *History of England* (1754–1762) brought him both fame and financial stability. He also served as librarian of the Faculty of Advocates in Edinburgh and later as undersecretary of state (1767–1768). After several stays in France and a long public career, Hume retired to Edinburgh, where he died in 1776.

In his brief autobiography, edited by his friend Adam Smith, Hume portrayed himself as a cheerful, sociable, and good-humored individual, undeterred by the setbacks that marked his early intellectual life. His *Dialogues Concerning Natural Religion*, written earlier but published posthumously, would become one of the most influential works in the philosophy of religion.

Today, Hume is recognized as one of the most important philosophers of the modern era. By drawing out the full consequences of empiricism across epistemology, ethics, religion, aesthetics, and social philosophy, he reshaped the philosophical landscape and profoundly influenced subsequent thinkers. Understanding his philosophy requires not only familiarity with individual arguments, but an appreciation of the unified vision of human nature that underlies his work — a task to which this book is devoted.

THE PROBLEM OF KNOWLEDGE

Before addressing questions concerning morality, religion, society, or human nature, David Hume begins with a more fundamental issue: the problem of knowledge. What can human beings know, how do they come to know it, and what are the limits of their understanding? For Hume, these questions are not abstract puzzles detached from life, but the necessary starting point for any serious philosophical inquiry.

Philosophical reflection on knowledge seeks to clarify the origin and nature of what we know, the extent to which human reason is capable of attaining truth, and the degree of objective validity that can be attributed to our beliefs. It also asks where knowledge reaches its limits—where certainty gives way to probability, and where reason must acknowledge its own boundaries. These concerns form the core of what is traditionally known as the theory of knowledge.

From a classical perspective, the problem of knowledge rests on two fundamental assumptions. First, knowing is understood as a human activity and can therefore be examined in a general and systematic manner. Second, the immediate object of knowledge is not external reality itself, but ideas—mental contents that appear within consciousness. The central question then becomes whether these ideas correspond to anything beyond the mind and, if they do not, how we are to distinguish reliable knowledge from illusion or error.

Hume's originality lies in the way he approaches these questions. Rather than beginning with abstract principles or metaphysical claims about reality, he turns his attention to human experience itself. In doing so, he places the investigation of knowledge firmly within the domain of empirical observation and human psychology. To understand Hume's theory of knowledge, it is therefore essential to examine the empiricist framework within which his philosophy is developed.

Empiricism in the Theory of Knowledge

For Hume, knowledge consists in the set of ideas in the mind concerning the beings of the world, ideas that are the product of impressions received through the senses. The mind is thus the subjective space, an inner theater in which perceptions appear successively, combine with one another, and disappear. It is not, however, a specific place in which these processes occur; rather, the mind is constituted by the very set of perceptions themselves.

Knowledge, moreover, can have its foundation only in experience and observation. This is the fundamental principle affirmed by empiricism, the philosophical tradition within which Hume situates himself.

The essential characteristics of empiricism, in contrast to rationalism,[2] are the following: the admission of a single method of knowledge, the inductive method, which proceeds from experience; the denial that the mind contains innate ideas or abstract concepts, such that knowledge is reduced to sensory impressions and ideas, which are faint copies of those impressions; the claim that sensory qualities are subjective; the reduction of relations between ideas to associations that, when they become habitual, are taken to be principles, such as causality; and the limitation of knowledge to phenomena, which renders impossible all metaphysics understood as the study of matters inaccessible to the understanding and as the search for a foundation of existence beyond the material world.[3]

Theory of Ideas

Hume's theory of ideas is a genetic theory, in the sense that, from his perspective, we understand the human mind and why we think as we do by discovering the origins of ideas, which together constitute knowledge.

Hume maintains that everything that can be known, everything that is present before the mind, consists of perceptions; thinking, therefore, consists in the occurrence or production of these perceptions. Perceptions may be of two kinds, if we consider their degree of intensity: impressions, which are vivid, forceful, and lively (including sensations, passions, and emotions), and ideas, which are faint images of impressions (arising in thought or reasoning and possessing little intensity). To think, then, is to bring ideas into play in reasoning; it is, quite simply, to order ideas.

For Hume, all the ideas present in the mind are copies of corresponding impressions, and there is no case in which the reverse occurs. When doubt arises regarding this claim, Hume challenges his interlocutors to produce a counterexample. Here his skepticism becomes evident, though not in the radical Pyrrhonian sense:[4] it requires recognition of the limits of human knowledge and of the impossibility of attaining absolute truth.

To clarify this form of skepticism, it is worth recalling that the name of this epistemological position derives from the Greek *sképtomai*, meaning "to look carefully." On this view, there is no firm knowledge or secure opinion to which one can definitively adhere, and judgment must therefore be suspended. Pyrrho, the Greek philosopher of classical antiquity, took this stance to an extreme by affirming that sensory impressions themselves are unreliable, making judgment impossible. Another skeptical thinker, Sextus Empiricus,[5] by contrast, accepted phenomena[6] and held that they can be observed, studied, and acted upon. This more moderate form of skepticism—known as phenomenalism—is shared by Hume, for whom human knowledge is limited and thus yields certainty only within experience, not access to absolute truth.

Phenomenalism admits nothing that is not evident, and what counts as evident is the phenomenon itself; nothing else meets this criterion. Hume therefore holds that we cannot know the substance or ultimate foundation of things, nor can we know any necessary connection between phenomena, since experience provides no corresponding idea. What we can know are only the particular qualities immediately given to the senses.

Perceptions may also be classified according to their divisibility into simple perceptions (those that admit no distinction or separation) and complex ones (those that can be divided into parts). Every complex idea can be decomposed into simple ideas, and to each simple idea there corresponds a simple impression.

Just as perceptions can be distinguished, impressions can also be divided into impressions of sensation and impressions of reflection. Impressions of sensation arise immediately in the mind in an unknown manner, since we do not know the source of the information provided by the senses. Impressions of reflection, by contrast, derive from ideas and consist in passions or emotions. When we reflect on an idea, an impression is produced that does not originate in the external senses but in an internal operation of the mind.

Within this context appear beliefs, understood as responses of the mind to sensory experience.

Impressions are actualized in the mind and may reappear through memory or imagination. Memory is the faculty by which we reproduce impressions in the mind with a relatively high degree of vividness, preserving the order in which the original objects and impressions were presented. Imagination, by contrast, is not bound to preserve either the order or the form of the original impressions; it has the freedom to rearrange and transform ideas, thereby giving rise to fantastical ideas composed of simple impressions.

The operations of the imagination, however, are not chaotic. There are certain characteristics or natural dispositions that Hume calls natural relations, which regularize and structure its activity. For these relations to operate, a stimulus provided by impressions of sensation is required. They may be understood as a gentle force that leads the mind from one determinate perception to another. These natural relations are dispositions shared by all human beings, although their causes are entirely unknown. They are not infallible, since one can fix attention on an object without passing beyond it, without one idea or impression introducing another. Hume identifies three such natural relations: resemblance (one object leads us to another, as when a painting calls to mind the original scene because of their similarity); contiguity (the relation of nearness in space or time, as when locating a house naturally directs us to nearby points of reference); and causality (the relation that generates the strongest connection, whereby thinking of an object—such as an axe—inclines us to think both of its origin, the blacksmith, and of its effects, such as cutting wood).

In addition to natural relations, there are philosophical relations, which allow us to compare ideas voluntarily. These relations are arbitrary, in the sense that they are established by human beings, since the mind is not naturally compelled to move from one perception to another. Hume identifies seven such relations: resemblance, identity, relations of time and space, proportion in quantity or number, cause and effect, degrees of quality, and contrariety.

Analysis of Causality

Causality is the most important of the natural relations, for it allows us to draw inferences from one object to another that go beyond sensory impressions and memory. It is the foundation of all reasoning concerning matters of fact.

When we think of a wound, it seems natural to ask what produced it, what occasioned it. If a billiard ball is set in motion, it likewise appears necessary to consider what originated that movement. Yet Hume rejects the view that everything that begins to exist must necessarily have a cause.

Why does he make this claim? First, he argues that the principle is neither intuitively certain nor demonstrative. It is not intuitively certain because it is not grounded in any of the philosophical relations that constitute relations of ideas. Nor is it demonstrable, since we can, at a given moment, conceive of something as nonexistent—or be entirely unaware of its existence—and then later conceive it as existing, without thereby conceiving a cause. If such a separation between an object and its supposed cause is conceivable, then the connection between them is not necessary. Moreover, whatever we can conceive implies no contradiction and is therefore possible: it may occur or not occur without logical inconsistency. For this reason, no necessity can be established through ideas alone; experience is required.

We are therefore led to conclude that the principle that "everything that begins to exist must have a cause"[7] must have its origin in experience. Yet experience itself shows that no object, considered in isolation, implies the existence of another. If we analyze an object in itself, attending only to the qualities presented to the senses, we find nothing that reveals either its causes or its effects.

What we initially perceive is merely the conjunction of two objects: they are contiguous, and one succeeds the other in time. Beyond this, however, we perceive no quality that binds one object to the other. We see only that one follows the other. The question thus becomes: where does the idea of causality originate?

According to Hume, the constant conjunction of two objects gives rise to habit. When one object appears, we come to expect the appearance of another. Past experience leads us to anticipate similar outcomes in the future. The two objects are related by contiguity, which makes them appear together, and by succession, whereby one follows the other. Yet even repeated examination of the objects themselves never reveals their causes or effects.

Causality, then, is not discovered in the objects but is established by the subject on the basis of habit formed through constant conjunction, contiguity, and succession. The mind develops the belief—acquired through custom—that the future will resemble the past. We must therefore reject the claim that there exists a necessary connection between objects, such that one would be the cause and the other the effect.

To conclude this discussion, we may define what Hume understands by a cause: an object that precedes another, is contiguous with it, and is united with it in such a way that the idea of the one determines the mind to form the idea of the other. On this basis, inferences are possible.

But since every idea derives from an impression, we must still identify the impression corresponding to the idea of necessary connection. In observing objects, we never discover any quality that binds them as cause and effect; nothing in them suggests such a connection. Because the senses cannot provide an impression of necessary connection—there is no impression of sensation corresponding to it—we must seek its origin in an impression of reflection. One event appears conjoined with another, but not connected. The idea of necessary connection arises from the repetition of similar instances of constant conjunction. The transition of the mind from the representation of one object to that of its usual accompaniment is the feeling or impression from which the idea is formed. This feeling is the origin of the idea of necessary connection, which therefore arises from an impression of reflection, not from external experience but from an internal operation of the mind.

Human beings thus form ideas of objects, reflect upon them, and—on the basis of habit—come to regard one as producing another. Here lies the origin of the idea of necessary connection.

Domains and Degrees of Knowledge

In explaining causality, we have referred to the reflection through which human beings establish connections between ideas. It is necessary, however, to specify that this reflection always proceeds from objects present to the mind. All the objects of human reason and inquiry, Hume maintains, can be divided into matters of fact and relations of ideas, the two domains of knowledge. Causality introduces us to the study of matters of fact.

By matters of fact, Hume understands a domain of knowledge that depends entirely on experience. Here there is no demonstrative certainty, since the contrary of any experiential phenomenon—for example, that a stone released from the hand will not fall—is perfectly conceivable, and the mind encounters no difficulty in thinking it. Once we recognize that causality lacks a rational foundation and rests instead on belief, nothing guarantees that past phenomena will occur in the future. In matters of fact, therefore, the opposite of what we have previously observed always remains possible, since there is no necessity ensuring that events will recur in the same way. The certainty proper to matters of fact is grounded in experience, and the knowledge we have of these objects of human reason is merely probable.

Of the seven philosophical relations distinguished by Hume, three belong to the domain of matters of fact: causality, identity, and relations of time and space. They yield contingent knowledge, since these relations may vary without any change in the objects themselves. Matters of fact rest on experience, and for this reason the knowledge derived from them is contingent.

By relations of ideas, Hume refers to propositions that possess demonstrative certainty. They are discovered by the mere operation of thought, independently of what may exist anywhere in the universe. This is the domain of arithmetic and algebra. Because it depends solely on rational operations, it admits of demonstrative certainty and constitutes a more genuine form of truth than that of matters of fact, which is based on the relation of cause and effect—an arbitrary belief discovered not by reason but through experience.

Among the relations of ideas are resemblance, contrariety, degrees of quality, and proportions of quantity and number. Although they originate in experience, they subsequently become independent of it and allow us to attain truths through rational operations. Once such truths are established, their validity no longer depends on empirical verification: they are known through the mere operation of thought, by intuition, independently of whatever exists in the world.

These relations hold without requiring that the signs composing them refer to factual existents, since to deny them would involve contradiction. They are valid because they correspond to ideas themselves rather than to things. "Thus, in this (and only in this) sense," Hume maintains, "necessity and universality are possible." Here we find necessary knowledge, in contrast to the merely probable knowledge characteristic of matters of fact. Yet this necessary and universal knowledge has no formal value with respect to reality, since universal contents do not exist.

Idea of the Self (Personal Identity)

To speak of truths discovered by the mere operation of thought—those corresponding to relations of ideas—presupposes the existence of a knowing subject.

One might suppose that there is an idea of the self, that is, an impression we have of ourselves and of which we are conscious at every moment: the self understood as a substantial unity. Hume, however, rejects this claim. Since every idea must derive from a corresponding impression, we must ask which impression gives rise to the idea of the self. Such an impression would have to be invariably identical throughout the whole of one's life, for the self is supposed to remain the same despite changes in the person, such as alterations in appearance. Experience, however, shows that no such constant and invariable impression exists. The idea of the self therefore does not arise from any impression and, strictly speaking, does not exist.

Our impressions, in fact, are discontinuous. In order to conceal this discontinuity, the mind constructs fictitious ideas by means of philosophical relations.

Among these are the ideas of the self, the soul, and substance. The self is thus an invention—though one that can be described as a bundle or collection of perceptions, a fiction generated by the imagination.

Personal identity, then, is a quality we attribute to perceptions by virtue of the way their ideas are united in the imagination when we reflect upon them. It is the idea we form of ourselves as something invariable and continuous across what is, in reality, a succession of changing perceptions over time.

To speak of such fictitious ideas, to which the idea of the self belongs, along with that of substance, leads us to a further class of ideas that Hume likewise regards as fictions: abstract ideas.

Abstract Ideas

For Hume, general ideas are nothing more than particular ideas associated with a certain term that gives them greater extension and allows them, on occasion, to recall other similar individuals.

In forming most of our general ideas, we abstract from every particular degree of quantity and quality. Yet when we speak of an abstract idea, it seems to represent either all possible sizes and qualities of an object or none at all. It cannot represent all possible qualities, since that would require an infinite capacity of the mind. In order to form a notion of quantity or quality, the mind must have a determinate idea of their specific degrees. But the existence of such abstract ideas is impossible, since everything in nature is individual. It is therefore absurd to suppose that an object such as a triangle lacks determinate proportions of sides and angles. It is impossible to form an idea of an object that possesses quantity and quality without those attributes having precise degrees. From this it follows that no idea can be formed that is not limited and determined in these respects. Abstract ideas, consequently, are individual. The image present to the mind is always that of a particular object, even though its use in reasoning is the same as if it were universal.

When we recognize resemblance among several objects, we apply the same name to all of them, regardless of the differences we may observe in their degrees of quantity and quality or in other respects. Once this habit has been acquired, hearing the name revives in the mind the idea of one of these objects and leads the imagination to conceive it with all its particular features and proportions. Yet since the same word has been applied to other individuals that differ in many respects from the idea currently present to the mind, and since the word is incapable of reviving all those ideas at once, it merely "touches the soul," awakening the custom we have acquired in examining them. The word thus calls up a particular idea while also activating a habit that enables us to recall other particular ideas when required. We do not distinctly represent all such objects in imagination, though we could examine each of them separately if we chose to do so. The mind engages in a partial consideration, since it cannot produce all the ideas to which the same name applies at once. Nevertheless, no difficulty arises in practice from using some of these ideas rather than all of them.

When an idea is brought to mind and fails to refer us to all the others associated with the same term, we attribute this to an imperfection of our faculties, which can sometimes give rise to fallacious reasoning and sophisms. This problem arises especially in connection with abstract and complex ideas. We may therefore state the following: (1) whenever we employ a general term, we form the idea of an individual; (2) we rarely or never exhaust the total number of such individuals; and (3) the remaining individuals are represented through the habit by which we are able to recall them when the occasion requires it.

Such is the nature of abstract ideas and general terms. According to Hume, a particular idea becomes general by being attached to a general term—that is, to a term that, through customary conjunction, stands in relation to many other particular ideas and readily recalls them to the imagination. Since ideas are particular in nature and finite in number, they can become general in their representation, and encompass an indefinite number of other ideas, only by means of custom.

This position has a clear antecedent in the nominalism of the medieval thinker William of Ockham, who held that nothing is universal in itself, since universality has meaning only in relation to many things. Whatever is said to be universal with respect to other things is always, in itself, a singular reality. Ockham maintained that what exists in the mind is always something singular, and that there are no universals in the nature of things; universality is conferred by the subject through the intention of predicating something of many objects. The same view of abstract or universal ideas appears in Hume, in accordance with the theory outlined above.

The Idea of Substance

In the previous section we saw that abstract ideas consist in a term that encompasses particular ideas, and that custom brings these ideas before the imagination. The same applies to the idea of substance, which many philosophers employ as the foundation of their theories and whose meaning they often take to be clear. For Hume, however, the meaning of this idea is far from evident, and he therefore seeks to clarify it by asking about its origin.

If the idea of substance exists, it must derive from an impression; otherwise, as in the case of the self, we would have to conclude that it does not exist. Yet it cannot originate in an impression of sensation, since, if we ask by which sense we perceive substance, no answer can be given. Nor can it derive from an impression of reflection, which consists of passions and emotions, none of which can represent substance. Moreover, an impression of reflection would have to arise as a response of the mind to sensory experience, which is not the case here. The idea of substance is therefore reduced to a mere collection of simple ideas united by the imagination and designated by a particular name, through which we are able to recall that collection. The particular qualities that make up an object are referred to an unknown something in which they are supposed to inhere. It is clear, then, that for Hume the idea of substance is established arbitrarily in the mind.

Although the explanation of substance "in itself"—if such a thing truly exists—properly belongs to ontology, we have chosen to introduce the topic here because it concerns an idea found in the human mind, and thus requires an account of its origin. It has therefore been treated in this chapter only insofar as it is an idea.

Up to this point, we have examined, from Hume's perspective, what human beings can know and how they can come to know it. We have seen that knowledge is limited to perceptions and that the mind is capable of generating certain fictitious ideas, among which the most significant are those of the self and of substance. These ideas play a decisive role in human thought. Although they arise naturally and almost inevitably from the operations of the mind, their status becomes problematic once we ask whether they correspond to anything that exists independently of our perceptions. It is at this point that the problem of knowledge leads beyond epistemology and opens onto a new philosophical domain.

Among these fictitious ideas, none is more philosophically significant than that of substance. When substance is no longer considered merely as an idea produced by the mind, but as something that might exist in itself, we are led to questions concerning being as such. What does it mean to say that something *is*? And can human reason legitimately claim knowledge of being beyond the perceptions through which it appears to us?

BEING

Questions about being arise naturally once we recognize the limits of human knowledge. If all that we know consists of impressions and ideas, it becomes necessary to ask what sense can be given to notions such as *being, existence,* or *substance.* Do these concepts refer to something real beyond perception, or are they merely ways in which the mind organizes its experience?

It is in response to such questions that philosophy has traditionally developed the domain known as ontology. Ontology is concerned with being in its most general sense, whether finite or infinite, material or immaterial, and seeks to clarify what it means for something to exist.

Being and Existence

Although the ideas of being and existence, insofar as they are ideas, properly belong to epistemology, they are discussed here because Hume maintains that what we possess are ideas, whereas being considered "in itself" is not something we can know. What we actually have are impressions or ideas of objects that do, in fact, exist.

For Hume, the idea of being—commonly regarded as the most perfect of ideas—has its origin in the fact that there is no impression or idea of which we are conscious, or which we can recall, that is not conceived as existent. From this awareness arises the idea of being, which introduces us to the notion of existence. We never recall an idea or impression without attributing existence to it. The idea of existence must therefore either derive from a distinct impression accompanying every perception or object of thought, or be identical with the idea of the perception or object itself. Since every idea proceeds from a corresponding impression, it is evident that the idea of existence cannot be derived from any particular impression.

The idea of existence, then, is nothing other than the idea of what is conceived as existing. To reflect on a thing and to reflect on it as existent are not two different acts. When the idea of existence is joined to the idea of an object, nothing is really added to it, since whatever we apprehend we conceive as existent. Every idea we form is the idea of a being, and the idea of a being is simply any idea we form.

To oppose this conclusion, Hume argues, one would have to identify the distinct impression from which the idea of being is derived—something that is, in fact, impossible.

Traditional Metaphysics

Hume's assessment of traditional metaphysics[8] is decidedly unfavorable. He rejects concepts that have served as the foundation of other philosophical systems. Metaphysics, for example, has operated with the concept of cause, which Hume not only understands in a radically different way but also subjects to criticism.

He begins by examining how ancient philosophy treated notions such as substance, substantial form, and accident, explicitly referring to Peripatetic (Aristotelian) philosophy. We shall adopt some of these concepts here solely in order to highlight the differences introduced by Hume's system, without attempting to explain these doctrines beyond their literal meaning.

Aristotle held that every being requires certain conditions in order to exist, which he called causes.[9] These are of two kinds. Intrinsic causes, which are integral to the being itself, include the material cause (that out of which a thing is made) and the formal cause (that which constitutes a thing as what it is). Extrinsic causes, which determine a being from outside, include the efficient cause (that which brings another being into existence) and the final cause (the purpose or end for which a being exists).

Aristotle further maintained that the universe is a network of causes and effects, and that an infinite regress of causes is impossible. From this he inferred the existence of a first uncaused cause. Change or motion, on this view, is produced by the action of an efficient cause that functions as the source of movement.

Continuing his analysis of being, Aristotle distinguished two modes of being: substance (that which exists in itself and does not require another in order to exist) and accident (that which exists in another).

For Hume, however, these notions—cause and substance—are conceived in an entirely different way, as we shall see. He even characterizes them as fictions of ancient philosophy.

Substance or Primary Matter

We turn now to Hume's view of substance, having already explained his theory of causality. Since causality, as an idea established arbitrarily through mental association, does not exist in reality, it cannot serve as the foundation of being, as Aristotle maintained.

The ideas of bodies, according to Hume, are collections of ideas formed by the mind from various distinct sensible qualities that compose objects and that appear constantly united. We regard the compound they form as a single thing that remains the same through continuous alterations. The ideas of distinct and successive qualities are connected by a close relation, and when the mind observes their succession, it moves easily from one idea to another, perceiving no more change than if it were contemplating a single, unchanging object. This succession is thus taken to be a continuous object that exists without variation. The smooth flow of thought confuses the mind, leading it to attribute identity to a changing succession of connected qualities.

If, however, instead of considering the succession at successive moments, we compare two distant periods of its duration, we perceive variations that were previously imperceptible when the change was gradual. The apparent identity then dissolves, and the idea of diversity emerges. In order to reconcile these opposing perceptions, the imagination feigns something unknown and invisible, supposing it to remain identical throughout all these variations. This supposed entity is what is called substance, or primary and original matter.

A similar process occurs with the idea of the simplicity of substances. Suppose we consider a perfectly simple and indivisible object alongside another object composed of parts closely connected. When the mind contemplates them, there appears to be little difference, since the parts of the composite object are so strongly united that the mind passes easily from one to another, conceiving the combined qualities as forming a single thing. Yet if the object is considered from another perspective, its qualities are found to be separable and distinct. Since this reflection undermines the original conception of unity, the imagination again invents an unknown something—a substance or original matter—that serves as a principle of cohesion, allowing us to name the composite object as a single thing despite its diversity.

Hume further observes that when we attend to the imperceptible changes of bodies, we suppose them to share the same substance or essence. When we focus instead on their sensible differences, we attribute to each a distinct substantial form. To reconcile these two modes of consideration, we suppose that bodies possess both a substance and a substantial form.

According to Hume, however, the ideas of substance and substantial form are mere suppositions and have no basis in reality.

Accident

The notion of accident follows inevitably from this way of thinking about substance and substantial form. We find it difficult not to regard colors, sounds, and other properties of bodies as existences that cannot subsist independently and therefore require a subject in which to inhere.

Because we have never encountered these sensible qualities without simultaneously feigning an underlying substance, the same habit that leads us to infer a connection between cause and effect inclines us to infer a dependence of every quality on an unknown substance. This fiction, however, is no more reasonable than the former. Since every quality is distinct from every other, it can be conceived as existing separately—not only from other qualities but also from that unintelligible chimera called substance.

Moreover, since every idea must derive from a preceding impression, if we truly had an idea of substance, we would have a corresponding impression—which is impossible. An impression could represent a substance only by resembling it, but this cannot be the case, since the impression itself is not a substance and lacks the peculiar qualities attributed to substance.

Leaving aside questions about what may or may not exist and turning instead to what we actually know, Hume insists that those who affirm the existence of substance must identify the impression from which the idea arises. They must specify whether it is an impression of sensation or of reflection, whether it is pleasant or painful, whether it accompanies us constantly or only intermittently, and so forth. If they evade these questions by defining substance as that which exists by itself, this definition proves too broad, since it applies to anything that can be conceived and therefore fails to distinguish substance from accident, or the soul from its perceptions.

The notion of substance thus gives rise to difficulties that philosophers have been unable to resolve. If we follow these lines of reasoning, we might even conclude that our perceptions are substances, since each perception is distinct from every other and from anything else that may exist in the universe. Whatever is distinct is distinguishable, and whatever is distinguishable is separable by the imagination. Perceptions can therefore be conceived as existing separately—and in fact they do exist separately—without requiring anything else to sustain them. Yet this does not mean that they are the substance that grounds all reality. The inconsistency of such positions is thus revealed.

The External World and Bodies

Within the ontological question of what exists, something must be said about the external world, since human beings undeniably hold a belief in it. If we consider an object in itself, however, we find nothing in it that allows us to draw conclusions beyond the object itself.

In this way, Hume rejects every metaphysical attempt to ground being, a rejection closely connected to his critique of the principle of causality, on which metaphysical systems typically rely.

Hume therefore holds that it is ultimately pointless to ask whether bodies exist or not. We are naturally compelled to affirm their existence, even though this affirmation cannot be justified by philosophical arguments. Nature, he claims, has left us no alternative—perhaps because our reasoning faculties themselves are unreliable.

This conclusion does not lead to skepticism about everyday life, but it does impose clear limits on philosophical explanation. Once we acknowledge both the unavoidable belief in the existence of bodies and the inability of reason to ground that belief, the philosophical task shifts. Rather than asking *whether* bodies exist, we must ask *how* we come to hold certain beliefs about them and what these beliefs reveal about human understanding.

In particular, we are led to investigate the origin of our beliefs concerning the physical world: the belief in the continued existence of bodies, the regularity of natural processes, and the qualities we attribute to objects, such as space, time, and matter. These questions no longer concern being in itself, but the way the world appears to us through experience.

NATURE

Once the limits of metaphysical explanation have been acknowledged, philosophy turns toward the study of nature as it is given in experience. Human beings live in a world that appears stable, structured, and governed by regularities, even though reason cannot demonstrate the necessary existence of bodies or the ultimate foundation of natural order.

It is in response to this tension that Hume develops his philosophy of nature. Rather than attempting to penetrate the essence of things, he examines how human beings form beliefs about the natural world on the basis of perception and habit.

We understand by philosophy of nature the study of mobile being—that is, the study of the totality of beings that constitute the physical universe and the way in which they exist. According to what we have analyzed so far, the only means by which human beings can know objects is through perceptions: we have an impression of an object and from it form an idea. Yet in this part of Hume's thought his skepticism once again becomes evident. Since we cannot know anything beyond perceptions, objects "in themselves" remain outside our field of knowledge.

Belief in the Continued and Distinct Existence of Bodies

We noted earlier that Hume does not concern himself with the question of whether bodies or objects exist. Belief in the external world is the point from which every human being begins. Hume maintains that nature has not left this to our choice and has doubtless regarded it as too important to be entrusted to our uncertain reasoning: it would be futile to ask whether bodies exist or not. That is a point we must take for granted in all our reasoning.[10] However, it is still worth clarifying what a body consists in, even though we cannot rationally demonstrate its existence. For Hume, it is a collection of qualities related by contiguity, resemblance, and causality—relations that merely facilitate the passage of thought from one idea to another, without any necessary connection among them.

Hume observes a difficulty here: when we try to imagine a world of objects that exist permanently and independently of our perception, we find ourselves confined to the world of perceptions and unable to reach objects supposedly existing apart from them.

He argues that since nothing is ever present to the mind but perceptions, and since all ideas are derived from what is antecedently present to the mind, it follows that it is impossible for us to conceive anything specifically different from ideas and impressions. We may direct our attention outward as much as we like and chase our imagination to the heavens or to the utmost limits of the universe; yet we never take a step beyond ourselves, nor can we conceive any existence other than those perceptions that have appeared within that narrow compass. This is the universe of the imagination, and we have no idea except what is produced there.

Human beings therefore act as if bodies exist (though they cannot demonstrate it). All they can do is investigate the origin of the belief that bodies have (a) continued existence—that they continue to exist even when we do not perceive them—and (b) distinct existence—that they exist independently of our perceptions.

Hume considers three possible sources of this belief: the senses, reason, and imagination.

The senses do not give us an idea of the continued existence of objects, since they cannot show us that objects continue to exist when they are no longer present in experience. That would require the senses to keep operating after they have entirely ceased to operate, which is contradictory.

Nor can the senses explain the idea of distinct existence, which presupposes a distinction between subject and object. The senses deliver only a perception and never refer us to anything beyond it. A perception cannot yield the idea of a "double existence" (object and subject) except by an inference of reason or imagination. But once we move beyond what is immediately given, we are no longer speaking of the senses alone. We cannot say, either, that the senses allow us to distinguish ourselves from external objects, since drawing that distinction presupposes the idea of the self or personal identity; and, as we saw in discussing the theory of knowledge, that idea is itself produced by a fiction of the imagination.

Reason is not the source of these beliefs, either. Human beings tend to infer the existence of an object from the fact that they have a perception—and they often confuse the perception with the object. Such an inference, insofar as it purports to be rational, depends on the principle of causality. But causality, as we have seen, is arbitrary and without rational foundation. The belief in the continued and distinct existence of bodies, then, cannot be the result of reasoning, since it would rest on causality, which is itself a product of imagination.

Moreover, from the standpoint of philosophical reflection, everything present to the mind is a perception. The only way reason could infer the existence of something (continued or distinct) from something else (such as perceptions supposedly caused by external objects) would be through the relation of causality. Yet the idea of causality arises from the experience of constant conjunction between two things. Because what is presented to the mind consists only of perceptions, we can observe constant conjunction only among perceptions—never between perceptions and objects. No reasoning, therefore, can lead us to a conclusion about the existence of material objects. The fact that we have perceptions allows us to conclude only the existence of the perceptions, not of the objects.

The belief in continued and distinct existence is thus supplied by the imagination. Two notions that help explain how this occurs are constancy and coherence. We perceive something and later find that our perception is similar—for example, the next day—in relation to what we take to be the same object; it remains "the same" from one moment to another (constancy). And although it may change in certain respects, it does not entirely lose its order or pattern (coherence). Despite the differences among perceptions occurring at different times, we take ourselves to be dealing with an uninterrupted succession of similar impressions. To impose greater coherence and uniformity, the imagination generates the idea of continued existence, and with it the idea of "the same object," that is, identity. Identity is the idea of an object existing as the same at different times. Perfect identity is incompatible with change, yet experience shows that no object possesses perfect identity; we encounter only imperfect identity.

When there is an uninterrupted succession of exactly similar perceptions (not identical, but similar), the mind glides along by inertia and supposes that only time has changed. In reality, experience consists of momentary impressions, and we do not distinguish the members of the succession. Because of their resemblance, we believe we are dealing with one and the same perception, though reflection shows that they occur at different intervals and therefore are not the same. A contradiction emerges, and to relieve this perplexity the imagination constructs the fiction of a continued existence underlying the succession.

The idea of the distinct existence of bodies likewise calls for explanation. For Hume, the opinion of continued existence arises first and, without much study or reflection, brings the other along with it. The point begins from a basic premise: we conceive objects only through perceptions, and perceptions do not have a distinct and independent existence apart from the subject's mind. Hume illustrates this with an example: when we press one eye with a finger, objects immediately appear double, and one set seems displaced from its natural position. Yet we do not attribute continued existence to both perceptions; and since they are of the same nature, we plainly see that our perceptions depend on our organs and on the disposition of our nerves and animal spirits. Hume adds that the same conclusion is supported by the apparent increase and diminution of objects with distance; by apparent alterations in their figure; by changes in their color and other qualities during sickness; and by countless other experiments of the same kind. From all this we learn that sensible perceptions do not possess any independent or distinct existence.

If we conceive objects only through perceptions, and perceptions do not exist outside the subject, then the only way we can conceive objects is within the mind, not outside it. The only thing of which we are certain is our perceptions. This does not permit us to reach demonstrative conclusions about the independent existence of objects, since such conclusions would depend on the relation of cause and effect, which, as we have seen, has no rational foundation.

Nevertheless, the mind constructs a fiction: it attributes continuity to objects and grants them an independent existence. From the presence of a perception, it leaps to the affirmation of an object's existence. This is an illicit step; for that reason, the idea is a fiction, a product of imagination—just as the idea of continued existence was.

Although these beliefs in the continued and distinct existence of bodies are fictions, and although human limitation prevents us from passing beyond perceptions to objects, Hume nevertheless affirms—as we said at the beginning of this section—that we must accept the existence of bodies as something given by nature.

Space and Time in Bodies

If we are to speak of bodies, we must also explain certain concepts that help us understand how they exist, once their existence has been affirmed—namely, time and space (the ideas of duration and extension).

With respect to time, Hume holds that the idea is formed on the basis of the succession of ideas and impressions. Time, considered by itself, cannot present itself to the mind or be known. The experience of someone who sleeps and retains no notion of duration illustrates this point. Moreover, the mind has limits: certain motions escape our perception—for example, the propellers of a flying machine in operation, where we perceive only a circle, not the interval between successive perceptions, because our perceptions do not succeed one another with such rapidity.

From this it follows that time never appears to the mind either in isolation or as something accompanying an unchanging object. Rather, it presents itself in a perceptible succession of changing objects. The idea of time does not derive from any particular impression; it arises from the manner in which other impressions appear, without being a part of them.

We may conclude, then, that time is not a primary and distinct impression, but the manner in which different ideas, impressions, or objects are disposed as they succeed one another.

The idea of extension arises from the senses of sight and touch. Nothing that is neither visible nor tangible presents itself as extended. Extension is acquired in the following way: many bodies around us appear as visible or tangible, and when we attend to the distances among them, we form the idea of extension. Since every idea depends on an impression, we must ask whether the idea of extension depends on sensations from vision or on an impression of reflection. Because impressions of reflection are passions, it is clear that the idea of space derives from the senses.

When we observe an object, the senses transmit nothing more than impressions of colored points disposed in a certain order. Since the senses show us nothing beyond that, the idea of extension is merely a copy of these colored points and of the manner of their arrangement.

When we experience the same object with different colors, the disposition of the points remains constant. We therefore omit, as much as possible, the particular features of color and form an abstract idea consisting in the disposition of the points—their order and coincidence. Touch can confirm an object's disposition and thus corroborate the impressions received by sight.

In this way the origin of the idea of extension, or space, becomes clear. At the same time, we can identify other qualities bodies possess: what is visible or tangible presents itself as extended, and extension consists of several smaller impressions—finite, not infinite, and divisible—given to sight or touch, which Hume describes as impressions of atoms or as colored and solid corpuscles.

Only objects with these characteristics can be perceived by the senses. Bodies therefore present qualities such as color, solidity, the disposition or order of their parts, tangibility, and so forth.

Matter

On the topic of matter, Hume maintains that it is impossible to conceive a vacuum, or extension without matter, for a simple reason: if the idea of space is the idea of visible or tangible points arranged in a certain order, then we cannot form an idea corresponding to an impression that does not exist—as would be the case with something we neither see nor touch.

As for the nature of bodies, or the secret causes of their operations, Hume admits that he does not attempt to penetrate them, recognizing that such an enterprise exceeds the limited capacity of human understanding. He confesses that we can never claim to know body except by those external properties that present themselves to the senses. As for those who attempt to go further, he cannot approve of their ambition until he sees at least one instance in which they have succeeded. For his part, he contents himself with understanding as clearly as possible the way objects affect the senses and their connections with one another, as far as experience informs us of them. This suffices for the conduct of life, and it suffices for a philosophy whose aim is only to explain the nature and causes of our perceptions—that is, of our impressions and ideas.

At this point, the consequences of Hume's skepticism become fully apparent. His acknowledgment of the limits of human understanding is not restricted to our knowledge of bodies or natural processes, but extends to any attempt to go beyond what experience can provide. Wherever reason seeks to move past perception in order to grasp ultimate causes or necessary foundations, it encounters its own incapacity.

This limitation, however, does not lead Hume to deny the reality of the world or the regularities of nature. Rather, it invites a reconsideration of what human beings can legitimately claim to know and where philosophical inquiry must recognize its boundaries.

These same limits emerge with particular force when philosophy turns to one of its most traditional and demanding questions: the problem of God. Just as human reason proves unable to penetrate the nature of bodies or the ultimate foundation of natural order, so it encounters similar obstacles when it attempts to grasp the nature of an absolute and infinite being. The question is no longer merely theoretical, but concerns the very scope of reason itself.

THE PROBLEM OF GOD

Throughout much of the history of philosophy, God was regarded as the ultimate foundation of reality, knowledge, and morality. To understand the world, the human being, and the order of nature was therefore thought to require an understanding of the divine. Modern philosophy inherited this expectation, but also subjected it to unprecedented scrutiny.

It is within this context that the philosophical problem of God arises for Hume. Rather than approaching God through revelation or theological doctrine, he examines what human reason, operating within the limits of experience, can legitimately claim to know about a divine being.

The branch of philosophy traditionally concerned with such questions is known as theodicy. The term derives from the Greek *theodíkeia*, meaning the justification of God, and refers to attempts to defend the existence and attributes of God before the tribunal of human reason, independently of revelation.

Since knowledge—its possibilities and its limits—was one of the central concerns of modern philosophy, and of Hume's thought in particular, we shall pause to consider his position on the possibility of knowledge in relation to the problem of God, as well as the limits that such knowledge entails. In *Dialogues Concerning Natural Religion* and *The Natural History of Religion*, Hume sets out and examines several arguments advanced by other thinkers in an attempt to demonstrate the existence of God.

On the Existence of God

The *a posteriori* argument, which proceeds from effect to cause, maintains that the world implies the existence of an orderer. When we observe an object produced by human artifice, we infer the existence of a mind that designed it; by analogy, it is then claimed that a superior mind must have organized the totality of the universe. Hume rejects this argument, however, on the grounds that no legitimate analogy can be established between products of human manufacture and the world understood as the product of divine design. Causal inferences rest on the observation of a constant conjunction between two classes of objects—constant being the crucial term. Deprived of such experience, since experience alone reveals the true cause of any phenomenon, we find that the supposed relation between God and the world is unique, singular, and without parallel. As resemblance between cases diminishes, so too does evidential force. Hume observes that when we see two objects constantly conjoined, custom leads us to infer the existence of one from the other; but this inference is impossible when the objects in question are unique and lack any comparable resemblance. For this reason, we cannot infer that the universe bears a resemblance sufficient to justify, with the same degree of certainty, the existence of a similar cause. The dissimilarity between any particular object and the universe as a whole is overwhelming. Attempting to explain the universe on this basis would be like trying to understand the vegetative process of a tree from perfect knowledge of the flight of a single leaf.

Since human beings have only an imperfect knowledge of a small portion of the world, they are in no position to pronounce definitively on the origin of the whole. It is unwise to measure objects so vastly disproportionate by a single standard.

Hume's skepticism is evident when he affirms the impossibility of human nature forming any idea that corresponds, even remotely, to the ineffable sublimity of the divine attributes. We lack the data necessary to establish any system of cosmogony, since our experience—imperfect in itself and extremely limited in scope and duration—cannot provide even a probable conjecture about the totality of things.

Still less, Hume argues, is it legitimate to portray the deity in terms analogous to the human mind by attributing to it human sentiments such as gratitude, resentment, love, friendship, censure, pity, or envy. It is unreasonable to transfer such sentiments to a supreme being or to suppose that such a being could be influenced by them.

Another argument for the existence of God appeals to the principle that like effects arise from like causes. Yet accepting this principle in the present case would require abandoning the infinitude of God, since the cause would have to be proportionate to the effect. The effect, however, insofar as it falls within the sphere of human knowledge, is finite; finitude would therefore have to be attributed to God.

An *a priori* argument for the existence of God—proceeding from cause to effect—has also been proposed. This argument does not begin from contemplation of the works of nature, but instead asserts that everything that exists must have a reason for its existence, and that there must therefore be an ultimate cause that exists necessarily. This being, which serves as the ultimate cause, is said to contain the reason for its own existence and to be inconceivable as nonexistent without contradiction; this being is then identified with God. Hume rejects this argument by pointing out that nothing can be demonstrated unless its negation implies a contradiction. Yet whatever we can conceive as existing we can also conceive as not existing; there is no being whose nonexistence entails a contradiction. The notion of "necessary existence," he concludes, is devoid of meaning.

Hume does not deny the existence of God. This is clear when he states that no person of common sense has ever entertained a serious doubt about a truth so certain and self-evident as the existence of God. Elsewhere he adds that it is evident there is purpose, intention, and design in everything, and that when our understanding reflects on the first origin of the visible system surrounding us, we are compelled to adopt, with firm conviction, the idea of an intelligent cause or author. He likewise affirms that the whole frame of nature bespeaks an intelligent author. It would seem, then, that for Hume there is no doubt about the existence of a Supreme Being.

What Hume denies is our capacity to demonstrate that existence by rational means. The arguments advanced by other thinkers fail to convince him precisely because they exceed the limits of human understanding. To inquire into the creation and formation of the universe, the existence and properties of spirits, or the powers and operations of a universal spirit without beginning or end—omnipotent, omniscient, immutable, infinite, and ineffable—is to venture into matters that lie beyond the reach of our faculties. In theological reasoning, Hume suggests, we confront something too vast for our capacities. For this reason, he likens us to strangers in a foreign land, to whom everything should appear suspect.

There is, then, no difficulty in affirming the existence of God, but that existence cannot be demonstrated by rational argument, given the intrinsic limits of human knowledge. Human beings may acknowledge the existence of God, but they should not attempt to prove it, since such proof exceeds the bounds of reason and inquiry. It would seem that the only "evidence" available lies in the inexplicable order and artifice of nature itself. Indeed, Hume suggests that the sciences almost inevitably lead us, without our noticing it, toward recognition of a first intelligent author, whose supreme intelligence manifests itself in the perfection of nature. Setting aside any appeal to revelation, it remains of interest to examine how belief in such a divine being arises within human nature itself.

Religions

Historical inquiry, Hume argues, makes it clear that the earliest and most ancient form of religion is polytheism. The monotheism of one or two peoples does not constitute a significant exception to this rule. Before arriving at the notion of a Supreme Being, the masses entertained only crude ideas of higher powers, initially conceiving the divine as possessing limited faculties, organs, passions, appetites, and human features. Only later did they arrive at the idea of a deity conceived as pure spirit—omniscient, omnipotent, and omnipresent. As the mind advances from the inferior to the superior, it abstracts from the imperfect in order to reach the idea of the perfect. Starting from their own nature, human beings separate what they take to be their nobler qualities and transfer them, in a more excellent and refined form, to the divinity.

Primitive human beings did not speculate about the causes of phenomena or pause to contemplate them. Rather, they were alarmed or frightened by what was new or unexpected. The first stirrings of religion thus arose from concern for life itself: from human hopes and fears, the pursuit of happiness, fear of misfortune, terror of death, thirst for vengeance, hunger, and similar passions—not from contemplation of the admirable order of nature. For this reason, Hume maintains that the principles underlying religious sentiment are secondary, unlike basic affections such as sexual attraction or parental love.

Each phenomenon was assumed to be governed by an intelligent being, and since experience shows that phenomena often oppose one another—for example, storms destroy what the sun allows to grow—human beings set about offering sacrifices and prayers to different divinities. The origins of events in the world were hidden from them, and threats or evils could not be foreseen. In their attempt to represent these hidden causes, human beings imagined beings in human form, to whom they attributed passions, appetites, and bodily organs, while also endowing them with superior powers of will and intelligence. The representations of the gods arose from their incomprehensibility and invisibility, making images, statues, and other sensible representations necessary.

This polytheistic tendency gradually evolved into theism—the doctrine of a supreme deity, creator of nature. Among the many gods, greater worship came to be directed toward one, either because a particular nation was consecrated to it or because, by analogy with earthly sovereignties, one deity was thought to rule over the others. Devotees sought to offer it ever greater praise, and the more pressing human needs became, the more exalted the adoration directed toward it, until it reached the point of infinitude. In this way the notion of a perfect being and creator of the world emerged.

Hume observes that human beings, through their praise and their desire to exalt their gods, inflate the ideas they have of them; by elevating their deities to the highest conceivable degree of perfection, they eventually attribute to them unity, infinity, simplicity, and spirituality.

Yet even after reaching theism, there is a constant tendency to relapse into idolatry, followed by a return to theism—a continual ebb and flow. Once the idea of a single supreme being has been formed, its very inaccessibility leads human beings to seek intermediaries or mediators: subordinate agents such as demigods or saints, who participate in human nature and, being more familiar to us, become objects of devotion. From this renewed idolatry, the movement back toward theism occurs once again, following the same process already described.

The Divine Nature

Having examined the origin of belief in a single God, we are confronted with the problem of penetrating the divine nature itself. Although the existence of God may be regarded as a self-evident truth, we should not suppose that human beings understand the attributes of the divine being—attributes to which they ascribe every kind of perfection—or imagine that these perfections bear any resemblance or analogy to those of human creatures. We attribute to God wisdom, thought, providence, and knowledge because these are honorable terms within human language, and we possess no other concepts with which to express our reverence. Yet it would be mistaken to assume that our ideas correspond to divine perfections, or that God's attributes resemble the qualities found in human beings. God is infinitely superior to our limited understanding and should be regarded more as an object of worship in temples than as a subject of debate in schools. Our ideas do not extend beyond experience, and of the divine attributes or operations we have no experience. There is therefore nothing in human life or in the human condition that allows us to infer God's moral attributes or to know anything of infinite benevolence, infinite power, or infinite wisdom—attributes that are known only through the eyes of faith. What is truly absurd is to attribute human passions to the deity.

To know God, Hume suggests, is to worship him.[11] Any other form of worship amounts to superstition, which degrades God to the level of humanity—a being who delights in being entreated, solicited, offered gifts, and praised. Superstition, Hume argues, lowers God even further, portraying him as a capricious demon who exercises power without reason or humane concern.

In this context, Hume holds that those most deserving of compassion and indulgence are philosophical skeptics, who, aware of the limitations of their own capacities, suspend—or attempt to suspend—judgment on such sublime and extraordinary matters. For a well-disposed soul, the most natural sentiment in the face of this situation is to hope and desire that heaven might be pleased to dispel, or at least mitigate, this profound ignorance by granting humanity a more particular revelation—one that would disclose something of the nature, attributes, and operations of the divine object of faith.

Confronted with the impossibility of penetrating God's attributes, Hume inclines toward deism:[12] the view that there is no particular providence, and that the sovereign intelligence, having established the general laws of nature, allows them to operate without further intervention.

He summarizes his position by observing that a person who has a just sense of the imperfections of natural reason will embrace revealed truth with the greatest eagerness, whereas the arrogant dogmatist, convinced that he can construct a complete system of theology by philosophy alone, scorns any additional assistance and rejects extraordinary teachings. To be a philosophical skeptic, Hume concludes, is, for a man of letters, the first and most essential step toward becoming a genuine believing Christian.

The Problem of Evil

After addressing the problem of the existence of God and his attributes, it is necessary to consider the significance of evil within reality. The existence of the miseries of life is undeniable, and religious sentiment often arises from reflection on human weakness and suffering, which leads people to seek the protection of a supreme being. Yet the presence of evil in the world immediately calls into question the attributes commonly ascribed to God. If God wishes to prevent evil but cannot, this suggests impotence; if he can prevent it but does not wish to do so, this suggests malice; if he both wishes and is able to prevent it, then the question inevitably arises: why does he not do so? The problem is fundamental. Why does evil exist in the world? It cannot be attributed to chance, for it must have some source. Does it stem from divine intention? That seems incompatible with perfect benevolence. Is it contrary to divine intention? That would be incompatible with omnipotence. At this point, human reasoning reaches its limit. Nothing further can be affirmed, for these matters exceed our capacity, and the criteria by which we judge truth and falsehood no longer apply.

Here again we encounter Hume's skeptical conclusion: it is impossible to establish, by convincing arguments, the existence of God, his attributes, or the origin of evil. For this reason, he holds that the most reasonable attitude is that of the skeptic, who, in doubting, remains open to the possibility of a revelation that might come to the aid of limited human understanding.

We may conclude this chapter with a passage from Hume that captures the spirit of what has been said. He observes that the universal propensity to believe in invisible and intelligent power, if not an original instinct, is at least a constant accompaniment of human nature, and may be regarded as a kind of mark or stamp that the divine workman has set upon his creation. Nothing, he suggests, could more ennoble humanity than to be thus singled out from the rest of creation and to bear the image or impression of the universal Creator. At the same time, he laments how disfigured the deity becomes in human representations, and how much caprice, absurdity, and even immorality are attributed to the divine being.

Although human beings are unable to know the divine attributes or to demonstrate the existence of God by philosophical reasoning, this does not exhaust the significance traditionally attributed to religion. For many thinkers, belief in God has been regarded as the ultimate foundation of moral order, either through divine commands implanted in human reason or through moral precepts revealed by the Creator.

Hume firmly rejects this view. In *The Natural History of Religion*, he argues that neither fear of punishment nor hope of reward constitutes the true basis of moral behavior. Religion, and the divine will as it is commonly understood within it, cannot explain why human beings approve certain actions and condemn others.

If morality does not derive from divine command, the question becomes unavoidable: what, then, grounds moral distinctions? How do human beings come to judge actions as virtuous or vicious, admirable or blameworthy? To answer these questions, Hume turns away from theology and directs his attention to human nature itself.

MORAL PHILOSOPHY

Moral philosophy, as Hume understands it, begins not with abstract principles or transcendent laws, but with the observation of human conduct. Instead of asking what morality ought to be according to reason alone, Hume asks how moral judgments actually arise in human experience and what common features they share.

The task of ethics, in this sense, is to explain why certain qualities and behaviors elicit approval, while others provoke disapproval, and to identify the principles that govern human action as it is lived and evaluated in ordinary life. Moral inquiry thus becomes an investigation into the foundations of praise and blame.

In general terms, ethics—or moral philosophy—may be understood as the study of the end toward which human conduct ought to be directed and the means by which that end is achieved. Central to this inquiry are human actions insofar as we judge them to be good, and the principles on which moral life is founded. By morality we mean the set of norms or customs that govern a person's conduct so that it may be regarded as good; ethics, in turn, is the rational reflection on what constitutes good conduct. These elements will be examined here from the perspective of Hume's thought, drawing primarily on the *Enquiry Concerning the Principles of Morals*.[13]

Hume's ethical theory is generally classified as *teleological* or *consequentialist*, because it evaluates human actions in light of their ends and their effects. In this perspective, an action is not judged primarily by the intention behind it or by its conformity to a moral rule, but by the consequences it produces for human well-being.

The term *teleological* derives from the Greek *télos*, meaning "end" or "purpose," and refers to moral theories that assess actions according to the goals they serve. *Consequentialism*, closely related to this approach, holds that the moral value of an action depends on its outcomes rather than on abstract principles.

This position stands in contrast to *deontological* ethics, which centers on the notion of duty (*deon*, "what ought to be done") and maintains that certain actions are morally required or forbidden independently of their consequences. Whereas deontological theories ask whether an action conforms to a rule or obligation, Hume's ethics asks how actions affect human life, social harmony, and the sentiments of approval and disapproval that arise within experience.

Hume seeks to analyze the qualities and attributes that render human beings objects of esteem or contempt, as well as the habits and faculties that call forth praise or censure. His aim is to discover what estimable and blameworthy qualities have in common, and thereby to identify the foundation of morality—the universal principles from which approbation and disapprobation arise. To this end, he employs the experimental method, deriving general maxims from the comparison of particular cases. His ethical system is thus grounded in observation and fact. We shall then indicate the end toward which human conduct is directed and explain why his moral theory is considered consequentialist.

The Utility of Social Virtues

Hume begins by examining certain social virtues, such as benevolence, friendship, gratitude, civic spirit, humanitarian concern, and others associated with kind treatment and generous regard for members of our species. Much of the merit we ascribe to these virtues derives from the utility they provide, since society derives satisfaction and happiness from interaction with individuals who possess them. In a similar way, when we speak of an object—a plant, a tool, a piece of furniture—that confers advantages and produces benefits, we call it useful; conversely, when it fails to serve its purpose, it displeases us. Utility, then, plays a central role in moral evaluation.

Consider next justice, another social virtue. If human beings were naturally endowed with everything they needed and enjoyed goods in abundance, there would be no need for a division of property. Justice would be superfluous, since anyone who took possession of something belonging to another would leave the original owner undisturbed, given the absence of scarcity. Where nature bestows abundance, goods are enjoyed in common, without distinctions of right and property. At the opposite extreme, if we imagine a situation of extreme scarcity and constant conflict for survival, justice would likewise disappear, since it would become an obstacle to self-preservation. Justice, then, arises from its usefulness within human relations. Its function is to promote happiness and security by preserving social order.

From this it follows that public utility is the sole origin of justice. Justice exists because of the benefit society derives from its regular and strict observance. Both a condition of perfect generosity and one of complete rapacity would render justice unnecessary; our actual societies occupy a middle ground.

From this analysis, Hume concludes that utility is the sole source of the moral approbation we grant to justice, veracity, integrity, and other estimable qualities, and that it exercises a powerful influence over our sentiments. Hence his claim that "moral obligation is in proportion to utility." The good of humanity is the sole object of laws and norms, and common interest and the pursuit of utility inevitably give rise to distinctions between the just and the unjust. In everyday life, appeals to utility are constant. It should be emphasized, however, that the utility of virtue is not evaluated solely from an egoistic standpoint. To praise as virtuous only what benefits oneself and condemn what harms oneself would be absurd. We recognize virtue even in an enemy, when we admire a quality or skill despite its working against our own interests. Utility, then, is understood not merely with respect to oneself, but with respect to all those who benefit from the action we approve.

Humanitarian Sentiment

Moral obligation or moral sentiment, though grounded in utility, cannot be explained by self-love alone. There exists a more expansive concern for others, since the interests of society are not wholly indifferent to us. Utility is not always assessed in relation to oneself, and whatever contributes to the happiness of society naturally recommends itself to our approbation and goodwill.

Hume does not believe it necessary to inquire further into the origin of this humanitarian sentiment.

He treats it as a principle inherent in human nature, beyond which inquiry cannot proceed—a further expression of his moderate skepticism. What matters is the fact that no human being remains entirely indifferent to the happiness or misery of others. Humanitarian principles exert authority over our sentiments, leading us to approve what is useful to society and to condemn what is harmful to it. We are naturally inclined to prefer virtue to vice and the happiness of society to its misery.[14] Indeed, Hume famously remarks that "an absolute, unprovoked, disinterested malice has perhaps never had a place in any human heart." The merit of social virtues thus arises from this natural benevolence toward the interests of humanity. Sympathy and fellow feeling move us to praise or blame, as the spectacle of human happiness or suffering awakens pleasure or displeasure within us.[15]

In short, any conduct that promotes the good of the community is desired, praised, and esteemed by that community in virtue of the utility from which all benefit.

The Role of Reason in Morality

Hume rejects the view that morality is derived from reason, as well as the conception of moral duty as something taught through rational demonstrations of the beauty of virtue and the ugliness of vice. According to this latter view, moral distinctions arise from inferences of the understanding.

Against this, Hume argues that moral distinctions are rooted in sentiment rather than reason. Truths discovered by reason are, in themselves, indifferent: they produce neither desire nor aversion and therefore cannot motivate action. What is intelligible or evident elicits only the cool assent of the understanding. Hume aligns himself firmly with this position.

Reason's role[16] is to inform us of what is beneficial or harmful, both to society and to the individual who possesses a given quality or performs a given action. But reason alone does not generate moral approbation or censure. It reveals the tendencies of actions; humanitarian sentiment then favors those that are useful and beneficial. An example clarifies this point. In inanimate objects, relations similar to those found in moral agents may occur, yet we do not regard such objects as virtuous or vicious. A young tree may grow larger than the one from which it sprang and destroy it; if a boy were to grow up and kill his father, reason alone would treat both cases similarly. Yet we do not speak of a "criminal" tree. The ultimate ends of action are not determined by reason but by human sentiments and affections.

When we ask why a person avoids pain, no rational explanation can be given, since pain concerns feeling, not inference. Virtue is desirable because of the satisfaction it affords when sentiment is engaged. Reason, being cold and dispassionate, cannot motivate action; it merely guides impulses arising from appetite or inclination by indicating the means to attain happiness or avoid suffering.

Taste or sentiment motivates action insofar as it produces pleasure or pain, happiness or suffering, and thus becomes the source of desire and volition. This is the context of Hume's well-known claim that reason "is, and ought only to be, the slave of the passions," and can never aspire to any role beyond serving them.

For this reason, Hume insists that if all warm feelings in favor of virtue, and all aversion to vice, were extinguished—if human beings were rendered entirely indifferent to these distinctions—morality would cease to be a practical discipline and would lose all capacity to regulate life and action.

Considerations on Virtue

Virtue is distinguished from vice in that virtuous actions please or attract approval upon mere contemplation, whereas vice produces displeasure. An inanimate object cannot be virtuous, even if it possesses human shape or harmonious proportions, because it cannot arouse sentiments of esteem or love. Only human beings can be virtuous.

Hume identifies four classes of qualities that elicit moral approval: (1) qualities useful to others, such as justice, generosity, benevolence, and honesty; (2) qualities beneficial to the person who possesses them, such as prudence, industriousness, frugality, moderation, strength of will, bodily vigor, and intelligence; (3) qualities immediately agreeable to others, such as modesty, wit, courtesy, and decency; and (4) qualities immediately agreeable to the person who possesses them, such as self-respect, magnanimity, cheerfulness, dignity of character, and courage. Moral approval attaches to those qualities that are agreeable, and the good is fundamentally identified with what is agreeable.

Moral judgments, on this view, are infallible insofar as they rest on sentiments of pleasure and displeasure. What is noble, generous, and good moves the heart and inclines us to embrace it; what is base is naturally rejected.

The End of Human Conduct

From this perspective, it becomes clear why Hume's ethics is consequentialist. There exists a humanitarian sentiment common to all human beings, and the same object tends to awaken similar passions in all. This shared sensibility makes us receptive to virtues that promote the common good. That common good constitutes the end of human action. Human beings seek happiness—understood through the intertwined notions of utility and humanitarian sentiment—and in this sense Hume may be described as a eudemonist.[17] We sympathize with the happiness of humanity and recoil from its misery. As Hume states, "the ultimate end of all human industry is the attainment of happiness."

Ethics is therefore teleological: human actions tend toward happiness and the common good, not merely individual advantage.

The Development of Hume's Ethical Thought

In the Treatise of Human Nature, Hume sometimes suggests that the objects of moral approbation are those qualities that are immediately pleasant or productive of pleasure, implying an identification of the good with the pleasant and grounding moral distinctions in pleasure and pain.[18] This has led some interpreters to attribute a fundamentally egoistic[19] or even hedonistic orientation to his ethics. Hume does recognize egoism as a component of human nature, but he never regards it as the foundation of morality.

Later interpretations emphasize the shift from the *Treatise* to the *Enquiry*, where egoism becomes secondary rather than foundational. Experience itself shows that we are capable of approving justice and disinterested benevolence directed solely toward the good of others. Human beings cannot remain indifferent to one another, since they necessarily live among others.

Individual well-being is inseparable from collective well-being.

Accordingly, commentators have argued that the foundation of morality, for Hume, lies in a universal humanitarian principle shared by the entire species, producing broadly uniform sentiments of approval and disapproval.[20] Egoism is never presented as the true motive of moral conduct.

In this sense, Hume's moral theory presents a humane, beneficent, and even cheerful view of human conduct. Moral approval does not arise from fear, coercion, or obedience to abstract rules, but from sentiments that naturally incline human beings toward the happiness and well-being of others.

These conclusions, however, presuppose something fundamental about human nature: that human beings are not isolated individuals, but essentially social creatures. Moral virtues and vices would lose their meaning if there were no others affected by our actions, no shared context in which conduct could be useful or agreeable.

If morality is rooted in sentiments that arise within social interaction, then a full account of Hume's ethics requires an examination of society itself. How do human beings come together? What makes social life possible? And how do social institutions emerge from human needs and dispositions?

LIFE IN SOCIETY

Human beings are born into society. Their actions affect others and are, in turn, affected by them. Far from being a secondary or artificial addition to human life, social relations constitute the very framework within which moral sentiments, cooperation, and shared practices develop. It is within this context that Hume's social philosophy takes shape. Rather than explaining society through abstract contracts or purely rational designs, he seeks to understand it as the result of human weakness, need, and mutual dependence.

Social philosophy examines the conditions that make human society possible. In this chapter we shall present Hume's conception of the social dimension of human beings, as well as his account of social institutions—since these form an integral part of society—such as the state or government, and the relationship government bears to society. Finally, we shall outline the type of government Hume regards as most appropriate. Our point of departure, then, is society itself and its origin.

The Origin of Society

Unlike other animals, which nature has equipped with the means to satisfy their needs, human beings are characterized by weakness and want. Because need and fragility are joined in human nature, people must unite in society in order to compensate for their deficiencies, achieve parity with other creatures, and even attain superiority over them. Through society, individual weaknesses are remedied. By combining his strength with that of others, a person can undertake projects beyond his solitary powers; the division of labor increases skill in the arts; and mutual assistance provides protection against accident and misfortune. Only within society can human needs be satisfied, including the new needs that society itself generates.

It is thus utility that leads human beings to organize themselves socially. The advantages of society are clear: it remedies individual weakness in carrying out significant tasks; it increases power through the conjunction of forces; it enhances productivity through the division of labor; and it reduces exposure to chance and accident through mutual aid. In short, society provides strength, security, and skill.

Yet there must be some principle by which human beings first become aware of these advantages—a principle that constitutes the true origin of society, since explicit calculations of personal advantage lie beyond the reach of uncultivated individuals. Hume locates this principle in natural inclination. The sexual appetite unites human beings and sustains their union until a new bond arises in concern for offspring. This gives rise to the relationship between parents and children, in which parents govern through strength and virtue.

Custom and habit then act upon children, gradually making them aware of the advantages of social life. Once human beings, through early education, recognize the benefits of living together and acquire a taste for company and conversation, they also become aware of a disturbance that arises within society from the possession of external goods—those acquired through labor.[21] These goods must be protected, just as the body must be protected, and this protection is achieved through a convention in which all members of society participate. This convention stabilizes possession and allows each person to enjoy what he has acquired by labor or chance. Here lies the origin of justice, understood as respect for the possessions of others guaranteed by social agreement.

Hume observes that it is in each person's interest to leave others in possession of their goods, provided they act in the same way toward him. Each individual is aware of a similar interest in regulating his conduct. This convention does not take the form of an explicit promise;[22] rather, it consists in a general sense of common interest, communicated among all members of society and inducing them to regulate their behavior by certain rules. Once this convention is established, the notion of property arises: property consists of those goods whose stable possession is secured by the laws of society.

Certain circumstances give rise to property once society is formed. The most obvious is present possession, whereby individuals agree to regard as their own what they already enjoy. Others include occupation (what one possesses by being the first to occupy or discover it) and accession (what becomes one's own by being closely connected to existing possessions). These principles, however, depend largely on chance. Since such contingencies offer no firm foundation, a more stable principle of distribution becomes necessary: the transfer of property by consent, whereby possession passes to another only with the owner's agreement.

Hume summarizes these arrangements in what he calls the three fundamental laws of nature: the stability of possession, the transfer of property by consent, and the performance of promises. Together, these rules secure peace and cooperation within society.[23]

Once the rule of stable possession is established, it becomes evident that it is neither abstruse nor difficult to conceive. Society is not the accidental product of a long historical process; rather, the first condition of human beings was already social, with the rudiments of justice appearing in paternal authority exercised over children to preserve harmony among them. There was no original "state of nature" understood as a historical period of savage isolation prior to society. Such a state is a fiction. Even so, although the earliest human condition was social and contained the seeds of justice, the rules that guarantee peace and security are not always observed. This fact leads us to the origin of government, which arises as a remedy for the instability produced by violations of those rules.

The Origin of Government

Human nature inclines individuals to pursue their own interests, even though they also extend concern beyond themselves, especially toward friends and acquaintances. This tendency can lead people to seek immediate advantage at the expense of social order, committing injustices such as the wrongful appropriation of property. To preserve justice, define equitable rules, punish transgressions, and restrain fraud and violence, it becomes necessary to establish certain individuals whose task is to enforce justice. These are civil magistrates, governors, legislators, and rulers. Thus, arises civil government.

The primary and fundamental aim of government, according to Hume, is the administration of justice: the protection of property and the enforcement of contracts. Beyond this, government also undertakes large-scale projects beneficial to society, which individuals cannot or will not pursue on their own. Its functions therefore extend beyond mere surveillance of order.

Once human beings recognize the necessity of government for maintaining peace and enforcing justice, it is natural for them to assemble, appoint magistrates, define their powers, and promise obedience. Just as social trust depends on keeping promises, social order depends on obedience to civil authority. This duty of obedience, however, does not arise from any original contract. Government does not originate in a formal pact or in patriarchal authority, but rather in the authority of military leaders or chiefs whose effective command in times of conflict proved beneficial. The utility of their authority led people voluntarily to accept it. Government, therefore, does not rest on an explicit contract.

Obedience to Civil Government and Legitimacy

The duty of obedience to civil government does not, in Hume's view, derive in any way from an explicit promise made by subjects. Rather, it arises from utility, from common interest. That interest consists above all in security and protection, benefits that can be obtained only within a political society and not in a condition of complete independence. Hume maintains that the obligation of obedience must cease when the interest that sustains it ceases. If the people's interest is gravely affected by an intolerable government, they are no longer bound to submit to its authority. Such resistance, however, is justified only in cases of extreme tyranny and oppression. As long as a government fulfills its fundamental purpose—maintaining order and safeguarding common interests—the general rule must be one of firm obedience and, as Hume himself puts it, a kind of blind submission to authority.

Once human beings have become accustomed to obedience, they rarely think of departing from a path long followed by themselves and their ancestors. Habit thus plays a decisive role in consolidating obedience to government.

Given that this obedience lends authority to those who govern, it becomes necessary to ask who should be regarded as a legitimate magistrate. The first foundation of political legitimacy lies in prolonged possession of power, regardless of the particular form of government.

It is very likely, Hume observes, that the earliest form of government in any nation originated in usurpation; yet time confers solidity on such authority and gradually reconciles people to it, making it appear just and reasonable. Where prolonged possession is lacking, present possession alone may suffice to confer legitimacy, even if power has not been exercised since ancient times.

Hume argues that no maxim is more convenient than that of submitting to the government one finds already established in the country where one happens to live, without inquiring too scrupulously into its origin or first establishment. Few governments, he notes, could endure such rigorous examination. How many governments exist today, and how many more do we encounter in history, whose rulers have no better foundation for their authority than present possession?

A third source of legitimate sovereignty is conquest, which is often accompanied by admiration and glory, in contrast to the resentment usually directed at usurpers. A fourth source is the right of succession, whereby authority is transmitted by inheritance. Finally, authority may be grounded in positive laws, where legislation itself determines a particular form of government and the rules of succession.

Once the question of legitimate authority has been addressed, it is appropriate to consider which form of government Hume regards as most suitable.

Other Considerations on Government

When a system of government, whether real or hypothetical, is divided into different bodies or orders, it is necessary to consider the interests of each. If the interest of each body coincides with the public interest, the government may be judged wise and stable. If, on the contrary, these interests are not properly regulated or oriented toward the common good, the government will tend toward disorder and tyranny.

In a monarchy, power is concentrated in a single person, such as a king or minister, whose character may vary greatly in ambition, ability, courage, and temperament. This concentration makes the regulation of authority more difficult. In a republic, by contrast, authority is distributed among assemblies or senates, allowing for checks and balances that render the exercise of power more orderly and limit abuses—an advantage not easily achieved in monarchical systems. For this reason, Hume does not regard monarchy as the most adequate form of government for society, particularly for Britain, the political context in which he was writing.

In his essay *Idea of a Perfect Commonwealth*, Hume proposes dividing the territory into counties, each electing a representative. Those representatives would then elect a number of county magistrates and a smaller group of senators.[24] The senators would hold executive power, decide on war and peace, issue orders to public officials, and exercise prerogatives comparable to those of a king. Legislative power would belong to the county representatives. Additional magistrates would oversee religion, the militia, the administration of justice, and other public matters. Although Hume elaborates this institutional design in considerable detail, it is sufficient here to note that he clearly inclines toward a representative form of democracy,[25] despite living under a monarchical regime whose limitations and deficiencies he recognized.

Our analysis has thus moved from the origin of society to the establishment of political institutions, and finally to the form of government Hume considers most conducive to social well-being. These elements together define the core of his social philosophy.

It should be clarified, finally, that Hume's political principles align with those of classical liberalism. The state is conceived as minimal, with functions primarily limited to guaranteeing order and justice, though not entirely exempt from undertaking public works or development projects for the common benefit. Liberalism—characteristic of the Enlightenment, as noted earlier—maintains the idea of natural rights, that is, norms owed to human beings simply by virtue of their nature. It also privileges the individual as an agent who acts according to interests. In Hume's case, however, these interests are not purely self-regarding, since they extend to others through the principle of benevolence.

Up to this point, we have gathered the main features that Hume considers essential for understanding human beings as social agents. We have examined the conditions that make social life possible, the emergence of institutions, and the role that cooperation and utility play in sustaining human communities.

Yet throughout this inquiry, other fundamental characteristics of human beings have also come into view: the capacity for knowledge through perceptions, the impossibility of transcending those perceptions in understanding the world, the relationship human beings bear to divinity, and the foundations of moral action. Considered together, these elements point beyond any single domain of inquiry and call for a more comprehensive account of human nature itself.

To bring these dimensions together into a unified perspective, it is necessary to consider the human being not merely as a knower, a moral agent, or a social participant, but as the subject in whom all these aspects are integrated. This task belongs to philosophical anthropology, which Hume regarded from the outset as the overarching science within which all other philosophical inquiries are included.

THE HUMAN BEING

At the center of Hume's philosophy lies a single guiding conviction: that all the sciences ultimately relate to human nature. Questions about knowledge, reality, morality, religion, and society are meaningful only insofar as they fall within human comprehension and are assessed according to human faculties and capacities. To understand philosophy, therefore, one must first understand the human being who philosophizes.

It is from this perspective that philosophical anthropology emerges as the culminating point of Hume's system. Rather than seeking an immutable essence of humanity, Hume approaches the human being as a complex unity whose characteristics can be grasped only through experience and observation.

Philosophical anthropology is the branch of philosophy that considers the human being (*anthropos*) as its object of study from a comprehensive perspective. As philosophical reflection, it analyzes the foundations of the very notion of the human being and treats it as the starting point for all knowledge of ourselves and of the world. For this reason, Hume maintains that all the sciences relate, to a greater or lesser degree, to human nature and depend in some way on the science of man, since they fall within human comprehension and are assessed according to our faculties and capacities.

Philosophical anthropology, then, does not attempt to identify the features of some supposedly immutable human essence. Rather, it proceeds from the human sciences—physical anthropology, cultural anthropology, psychology, linguistics, sociology, and the like—in order to develop a reflection on the human being as a whole, explaining how the human being is the condition of possibility of those sciences and, more generally, of human conduct. For this reason, we present this discipline at the end of Hume's system, since it gathers together the knowledge obtained in earlier discussions. Hume himself maintains that since the science of man is the only solid foundation of all the others, the only solid foundation we can give to that science must lie in experience and observation. We must therefore glean our "experiments" from a careful observation of human life, taking human beings as they appear in the ordinary course of daily experience: in their mutual dealings within society, in their occupations and pleasures. This approach allows us to enter the domain of everyday life, from which we can extract the principal characteristics of the human being.[26]

The Human Being as Subject of Knowledge

We have already noted that, for Hume, every science falls under human comprehension and is judged by human beings. We can now take a further step: if human beings are capable of understanding and judging, it is because they are knowing subjects—that is, beings who possess ideas in the mind concerning the beings of the world, ideas that are the product of impressions derived from the senses. The mode of knowing, the contents of the mind (perceptions), and related matters have already been addressed in the theory of knowledge; here we shall confine ourselves to certain additional notions that clarify the human being as a knowing subject.

Hume remarks that human beings are capable of investigations of remarkable reach and depth: we may attempt to penetrate the nature of planets and celestial bodies, look back to the past in search of the first origin or at least the history of the human race, or project our gaze forward to consider the influence of our actions on posterity and the judgments that may be made of our character a thousand years from now. Human beings link causes and effects with great amplitude and complexity; they extract general principles from particular appearances; they benefit from their discoveries and, no less, learn from their failures, turning many errors to advantage.

These features allow us to characterize the human being as a rational creature. We shall return to the dimension of creature later; for now, we focus on what it means to call the human being rational. We have defined reason as the faculty by which we discern truth and falsehood, though Hume uses the term in several senses. Taking it in this basic sense, we can say that the human being is capable of knowing, forming inferences, and attempting to penetrate into things—while ultimately remaining limited to perceptions, which are the only objects of knowledge properly so called. Still, the human being can know, and this presupposes something like a mind, in which the activity of reasoning takes place.

The mind is the subjective "space" in which perceptions appear; and since perceptions are all that can be known, we encounter a rational being—one endowed with the faculty of reason—and a mind, understood not as a physical location within the body, but as an immaterial subjective field. It is not merely the place in which perceptions occur; it is the bundle or collection of perceptions themselves. Those perceptions are not material objects, since they are apprehended by thought or consciousness.

Other features of the knowing subject also make knowledge possible. Memory is the faculty by which impressions are repeated in the mind with a notable degree of vividness and in their original order. Imagination, by contrast, is the faculty that can alter the order of ideas and thereby generate fantastic combinations. Finally, the human being is equipped with senses—touch, sight, hearing, taste, and smell—through which perceptions are acquired. The senses are conduits through which impressions are transmitted, but they do not establish immediate contact between mind and object; for this reason, even though experience is the only accepted route to knowledge, the senses do not confer unlimited power.

The human being knows, then, through perceptions, which take the form of impressions and ideas. Among impressions of reflection, we find the passions—simple impressions not composed of more basic elements. This brings us to another dimension of human nature.

The Human Being as a Being of Passions

Hume distinguishes passions in human beings as direct and indirect. Direct passions arise immediately from good and evil,[27] in the form of pleasure and pain. Indirect passions, by contrast, derive from more complex principles of the mind and reinforce the direct passions. Among the indirect passions he includes pride, humility, love, hatred, benevolence, anger, pity, malice, envy, respect, contempt, and sexual love.

Pride and humility are opposed, and both relate to the idea the individual forms of himself, whether favorable or unfavorable. Pride is the agreeable impression that arises when contemplation of our virtue, beauty, riches, or power produces satisfaction with ourselves; humility is its contrary. When beauty or deformity is found in the body, these produce pleasure or displeasure and thus become causes of pride or humility; the same occurs with other bodily qualities, such as strength or vigor. Yet the source is not limited to bodily features. Whatever produces pleasure and delight—whether through utility, beauty, or novelty—may become a cause of pride, while whatever produces displeasure may become a cause of humility.

Love, Hume maintains, is directed toward a sentient and external being—that is, another person—in whom we discern virtues such as knowledge, wit, sound judgment, or good humor. Opposed qualities, by contrast, produce hatred and contempt. Here too, pleasure and displeasure function as indicators, directing us toward objects of love or hatred. Depending on whether one is moved by love or hatred, one forms a desire for the happiness or misfortune of the person who is its object; from this arise further passions such as benevolence, or its opposite, anger.

Pity consists in being troubled by another's misfortune, not only that of those we love. Malice consists in taking pleasure in the misfortunes of others, regardless of friendship or enmity. These phenomena are explained more fully through the principle of sympathy, which will be addressed in the next section. Envy consists in a diminution of our own pleasure upon considering the pleasure of another; another's superiority seems to diminish us and forces an unpleasant comparison. Respect and contempt arise from considering the qualities of others either as they are in themselves or by comparing them with our own. Sexual love, finally, derives from the pleasurable sensation produced by beauty, from the bodily appetite for generation, and from a generous affection or benevolence toward the object of pleasure.

Among the direct passions Hume includes desire, aversion, sadness, joy, hope, fear, despair, confidence, and related derivatives. When something agreeable is present, joy arises; when something is evil, sadness or sorrow follows. If the good is uncertain, hope is produced; if the evil is uncertain, fear arises. Desire proceeds from considering the good, and aversion from considering evil. When good or evil can be attained through some action of mind or body, the will is exercised—the internal impression, felt and conscious, that arises when we knowingly produce a new movement of the body or a new perception of the mind.

The passions, therefore, are the motive force of the will, not reason, as we have already explained. From this we may add another constitutive characteristic of the human being: liberty, understood as the power to act or not act in accordance with the determinations of the will.

In studying the passions, we also see that they are awakened by external objects—by what is taken to be good or evil, or by qualities possessed by others. Hume notes that he experiences passions such as hatred, resentment, esteem, love, courage, joy, and melancholy more through communication with others than through his own temperament. This leads us naturally to consider the human being in relation to other human beings.

The Human Being as a Social Being

In every society there is a profound interdependence among human beings, and almost no human action is entirely self-contained or performed without some reference to the actions of others. The human being is therefore a social being, governed in conduct above all by two general principles: egoism, the pursuit of self-interest, and altruism, the consideration of the interests of others in pursuit of one's own ends. As we saw in discussing Hume's ethics, egoism is indeed a feature of human nature, but it is no more fundamental than benevolence or the principle of sympathy.

Hume observes that no quality of human nature is more notable, in itself or in its consequences, than our inclination to sympathize with others and to receive, through communication with them, their inclinations and sentiments, however different—or even contrary—they may be to our own. We have already analyzed the nature of benevolence; here we consider certain consequences. From sympathy arises the broad uniformity of human action across nations and ages, which leads us to conclude that human nature remains constant in its principles and operations. The same motives have always produced the same actions. Ambition, avarice, self-love, vanity, friendship, generosity, public spirit—these passions, combined in different ways and distributed throughout society, have existed from the beginning of the world and continue to be the source of all the action and enterprise we observe. Humanity is so similar across time and place that, in this respect, history offers little that is truly new. Its principal utility is to reveal the universal and constant principles of human nature by presenting human beings in every variety of situation, and by supplying the materials for observation and reflection on the usual sources of action.

If a traveler returned from a foreign land claiming to have found human beings without avarice, ambition, or desire for vengeance, and knowing no pleasure other than friendship, generosity, and public spirit, we would conclude that he was lying.

The general observations gathered through experience provide the key to knowledge of human nature and teach us to disentangle its complexities. If there were no regularity in human action—if experience were wholly irregular—it would be impossible to accumulate general observations about humanity, and even the most careful reflection would be of little value. Yet this does not mean that uniformity extends to every detail. Human conduct varies with differences of character, prejudice, and opinion; and in no domain of nature is perfect uniformity found in all particulars. Moreover, human beings act with will and liberty. Still, observation of diversity allows us to form a richer range of principles, and these presuppose a degree of regularity sufficient to make the sciences possible, and above all the science of man, which for Hume includes the rest.

To complete our account of human nature, we must consider further characteristics. We began by describing the human being as a rational creature; having discussed rationality, the passions, and social life, we must now address what it means to call the human being a creature.

The Human Being and the Divine

For Hume, it is clear that God exists, though the natural limitations of human knowledge prevent us from stating what God's attributes are. Hume maintains that the order of the universe proves the existence of an omnipotent mind—that is, a mind whose will is constantly accompanied by the obedience of every being and creature. Nothing more, he suggests, is required to ground the essential articles of religion, nor is it necessary that we form any precise idea of the force and energy of the Supreme Being.

To speak of the human being as a creature is therefore to acknowledge God as creator, even though we cannot explain how creation takes place. Yet the relation human beings ought to bear to the deity is far removed from religious superstition. The most advisable attitude is simply to recognize God's existence: to know that existence is to worship; but we should not imagine a personal God who intervenes in the world, since the world is governed by general laws, and any further relation between God and the world is, at least for us, unknowable. In this sense, human beings are creatures; yet once created, they proceed according to their own nature, without appeal to divine intervention.

Closely connected to the question of divinity is the problem of the soul. The idea of a soul, if such an entity exists, appears to point to an immaterial element within the human being—one that would not be given in sensory experience and would therefore lie beyond the limits of empirical observation. For this reason, the soul seems to raise difficulties similar to those posed by the divine attributes themselves.

If human knowledge is confined to impressions and the ideas derived from them, as Hume maintains, it becomes necessary to ask whether we can form any legitimate idea of an immaterial soul, or whether this notion exceeds what experience can justify. The question is not merely speculative: it bears directly on how we understand personal identity, consciousness, and the persistence of the self over time. We therefore turn to Hume's examination of the soul and the arguments he advances in addressing this problem.

The Human Being and the Soul

There are philosophical positions known as dualist, which conceive the human being as a composite of soul and body. By contrast, there are monist positions, according to which the human being does not possess anything like a soul, but is only body. Hume belongs to this second view, as the following considerations show.

In certain passages of his work, Hume tends to equate the notions of soul and mind. He remarks, for example, that impressions of sensation arise in the soul without any prior perception. Yet impressions are themselves perceptions, and elsewhere he maintains that in order for perceptions to occur, the mind must begin somewhere. It therefore appears that the terms soul and mind are being used in the same sense, namely, to designate the set of perceptions or the subjective field in which they are found.

Later he affirms that bodily pains and pleasures arise originally in the soul—"or in the body, call it what you will"—without any preceding thought or perception. Here again, body, soul, and mind seem to be treated as interchangeable, as though no strict distinction were required among them. This suggests that Hume does not approach the human being from a dualist perspective. He also writes that when the soul applies itself to performing an action or conceiving an object to which it is not accustomed, there is a certain inflexibility of the faculties and a difficulty of the spirits in moving in their new direction.

In such passages, the soul appears both to perform actions, which would ordinarily be attributed to the body, and to conceive objects, which belongs to the mind or understanding. Hume thus establishes no clear distinction among these notions. From this it follows that he does not posit the existence of an immaterial substance called the soul that subsists beyond matter, or that continues to exist once the body has disappeared.

Hume nonetheless affirms that there surely exists a Being who presides over the universe and who, with infinite wisdom and power, subjects discordant elements to their proper order and proportion. He suggests leaving speculative reasoners to debate how far this benevolent Being extends his care, and whether he prolongs our existence beyond the grave in order to grant virtue its just reward and make it fully victorious. The moral individual, without pronouncing on so doubtful a question, is satisfied with the endowment assigned to him by the Supreme Orderer of all things. He gratefully accepts any future reward that may be prepared; but if it is not granted, he does not regard virtue as an empty name. Rather, considering virtue rightly as its own reward, he gratefully acknowledges the liberality of his Creator, who, in calling him into existence, has offered him the opportunity to acquire, if only once, so inestimable a possession.

We may conclude, then, that Hume conceives the human being exclusively from a corporeal—that is, material—standpoint. There is no underlying substratum called the soul that functions as a motor principle, nor any other mode of human existence to be realized beyond this life.

The Human Being as a Whole

In defining the discipline addressed in this chapter, we noted that its aim is to reflect on the human being in its totality, rather than from the perspective of a single faculty or isolated domain. Having examined the principal characteristics of the human being throughout the previous chapters—knowledge, belief, moral sentiment, social life, and the limits of reason—we are now in a position to bring these elements together into a unified account.

From Hume's perspective, the human being cannot be understood by appealing to an underlying metaphysical essence or an immaterial substance, but only by attending to the concrete features of human experience as it unfolds in ordinary life. The task, therefore, is not to construct an abstract definition of human nature, but to articulate a general notion of the human being as it emerges from observation, reflection, and the interplay of perceptions, passions, and social relations. It is in this sense that Hume's philosophy allows us to grasp the human being as a whole.

The human being is a creature of the Supreme Being, endowed with a body that enables him to exist and to know, without the presence of any substratum or soul functioning as a principle of life. This condition of being a creature does not imply dependence on God in the conduct of life: once the human being comes into existence, he develops according to his own nature, without recourse to divinity.

He is also a rational being, insofar as he possesses the capacity to discern, to know, and to infer. Yet reason is not the faculty that governs human conduct in daily life; rather, it is the passions that guide action, so that reason can only serve them.

The predominant passion, for Hume, is benevolence exercised in relation to others. For this reason, the human being is constituted as a social being. Human nature remains fundamentally constant throughout history, and the motives and actions of human beings in one epoch are, in their basic structure, the same as those found in human beings in another.

This continuity points to a human constitution that endures over time: a set of formal characteristics that remain stable without implying uniformity in every particular detail. These characteristics are developed at length in the three books of the *Treatise of Human Nature*, where Hume seeks to illuminate the nature of the human being—a topic that occupies a privileged place in modern philosophy.

With this account of human nature, the main lines of Hume's philosophical project come together. The inquiry that began with the problem of knowledge thus finds its completion in an understanding of the human being as the subject and measure of all philosophical investigation.

CONCLUSION

To conclude our examination of Hume's thought, it is helpful to recall the path we have followed. Beginning with the problem of knowledge, we have traced the limits of human understanding, examined the implications of those limits for metaphysics and theology, and explored their consequences for morality, social life, and human nature. What emerges from this trajectory is not a fragmented philosophy, but a coherent vision grounded in experience and attentive to the conditions of human life.

With respect to knowledge, Hume rejects the existence of innate ideas and principles, holding that all the contents of the mind arise from sensible experience. Philosophical investigation, therefore, should not lose itself in abstractions that cannot be accounted for in experiential terms. Hume's analysis of consciousness is commonly described as a psychological method, since it seeks to explain how knowledge is generated through observation and experience, taking impressions derived from sensibility as the primary materials of thought. From this standpoint, he adopts a skeptical position with regard to direct knowledge of objects, for human beings are confined to the realm of perceptions.

This same commitment leads him to reject notions that do not meet the criterion of empirical origin, such as the self, substance, and similar metaphysical entities. In this way, Hume becomes a penetrating critic of metaphysics, particularly of the traditional concepts of causality and substance. Yet if causality is reduced to constant conjunction, a further question arises: how are we to account for cases in which constant conjunction occurs without a genuine causal relation, or for situations in which a single event appears sufficient to ground a causal inference, as when the collapse of an empire is attributed to a specific war?

Hume extends empiricism not only to the theory of knowledge but also to the domains of theodicy and ethics, since he conceives morality itself as grounded in facts and observation drawn from common human experience and social life. In this respect, his application of the empirical method is radical. At the same time, it invites reflection on whether human beings—and reality more generally—can in fact be fully understood solely through the spatial and temporal conditions in which they appear.

In the realm of theodicy, Hume's critique of causality and substance directly affects the question of God's existence, since these concepts traditionally serve as pillars of religious metaphysics. Hume does not deny the existence of God, but he does deny the possibility of demonstrating it by rational means, thereby giving rise to a form of agnosticism. Even so, he remains open to the possibility of revelation, a position that in turn raises questions about the criteria for its validity and the conflicts that arise when different claims to revelation present themselves as exclusive.

Hume's philosophy also includes an aesthetic dimension, developed in his reflections on art and taste. He addresses such topics as literary genres, eloquence, the progress of the arts and sciences, and refinement of taste. Although these themes have not been treated in this book, it is worth noting that Hume understands beauty in terms of proportion among the parts of an object, a proportion that yields an agreeable end. Since what is useful is that which is suited to an end, beauty and utility are, for Hume, closely connected.

It should also be emphasized that the study of Hume naturally leads to an engagement with other modern philosophers upon whom his influence is unmistakable, as Kant himself famously acknowledged. More broadly, Hume's thought invites reflection on the consequences of setting aside the superhuman criteria that dominated medieval interpretations of reality in favor of an emphasis on the sensible world. One may ask what long-term effects this shift has produced, particularly in light of the recurrent observa-

tion that an excessive focus on the human can sometimes devolve into forms of inhuman or brutal behavior.

Many further consequences could be drawn from
Hume's philosophy, but they lie beyond the scope of
the present work. For now, it is enough to hope that
this book has achieved its aim of offering a general
panorama of David Hume's thought, one that may in-
spire readers to pursue a deeper engagement with the
work of one of the greatest thinkers of the modern era.

BIBLIOGRAPHY

PRIMARY SOURCES

Hume, David. *A Dissertation on the Passions; The Natural History of Religion.* Edited by Tom L. Beauchamp. Oxford: Clarendon Press, 2007.

Hume, David. *A Treatise of Human Nature: A Critical Edition.* Edited by David Fate Norton and Mary J. Norton. 2 vols. Oxford: Clarendon Press, 2007.

Hume, David. *An Enquiry Concerning Human Understanding: A Critical Edition.* Edited by Tom L. Beauchamp. Oxford: Clarendon Press, 2000.

Hume, David. *An Enquiry Concerning the Principles of Morals: A Critical Edition.* Edited by Tom L. Beauchamp. Oxford: Clarendon Press, 1998.

Hume, David. *Dialogues Concerning Natural Religion.* Edited by Dorothy Coleman. Cambridge: Cambridge University Press, 2007.

Hume, David. *Dialogues Concerning Natural Religion and Other Posthumous Publications.* Edited by M.

A. Stewart. Oxford: Clarendon Press, forthcoming.

Hume, David. *Essays Moral, Political, Literary*. Edited by Eugene F. Miller. Indianapolis: Liberty Fund, 1987.

Hume, David. *Essays, Moral, Political, and Literary*. Edited by Tom L. Beauchamp and Mark A. Box. 2 vols. Oxford: Clarendon Press, 2021.

SECONDARY SOURCES

Abbagnano, Nicola. *Diccionario de Filosofía*. Mexico: FCE, 1995.

Aristotle. *Metafísica*. Mexico: ESPASA-CALPE, 1986.

Bennet, Jonathan. *Locke, Berkeley, Hume: temas centrales*. Mexico: UNAM, 1988.

Brugger, Walter. *Diccionario de Filosofía*. Barcelona: Herder, 1978.

Camps, Victoria. *Historia de la ética*. Vol. II. Barcelona: Crítica, 1992.

Canals Vidal, F. *Historia de la filosofía medieval*. Barcelona: Herder, 1985.

Copleston, Frederick. *Historia de la Filosofía*. Vol. III. Mexico: Ariel, 1992.

Cortés Morató, Jordi, and Antoni Martínez Riu. *Diccionario de filosofía en CD-ROM*. Barcelona: Herder, 1998.

Ferrater Mora, José. *Diccionario de Filosofía*. Madrid: Alianza, 1986.

Fraijó, Manuel. *Filosofía de la religión*. Madrid: Trotta, 1994.

García Borrón, J. C. *Empirismo e Ilustración inglesa: de Hobbes a Hume*. Madrid: Cincel, 1985.

García de Oteyza, Mercedes. *La identidad personal en Hume*. Mexico: UNAM, 1984.

García Morente, Manuel. *Lecciones preliminares de filosofía*. Mexico: Ed. Época, 1981.

Hirshberger, Johannes. *Historia de la filosofía. Vol. II*. Barcelona: Herder, 1994.

Plato. *Diálogos. Vol. VI*. Madrid: Gredos, 1992.

Strauss, Leo, and Joseph Cropsey. *Historia de la filosofía política*. Mexico: FCE, 1996.

Verneaux, Roger. *Historia de la filosofía*. Barcelona: Herder, 1968.

Yvon, Belaval. *Historia de la filosofía. Vol. IV*. Madrid: S. XXI, 1973.

NOTES

1 The Modern Era begins with Descartes in the seventeenth century and extends to the eighteenth century with Locke, Newton, Leibniz, and Hume. These names stand as central figures of modern philosophy. Descartes emphasizes method; Newton, science; Locke, the theory of knowledge; Leibniz, metaphysics; and Hume, a new orientation of philosophy.

2 Denial of the value of experience for knowing, asserting that reason alone can attain evident truths.

3 Metaphysics means, etymologically, beyond the physical.

4 Pyrrho of Elis (360–220 B.C.), philosopher and founder of skepticism, affirms that it is not possible to know things, so we should suspend all judgment about them and remain indifferent.

5 Sextus Empiricus (250 A.D.) affirmed that one can observe appearances, establish relations, successions, and foresee, in order to act upon those appearances.

6 Phenomenon derives from the Greek *fainomenon*, that which appears.

[7] General maxim of philosophy, which is formulated by Plato, *Phileb.*, 26E.

[8] At the time when Hume develops his theories, the notions of metaphysics and ontology are used interchangeably.

[9] Cf. Aristotle, *Metaphysics*, A 3.

[10] This belief is known as common-sense realism.

[11] Hume has maintained the limitation of human knowledge and the impossibility of knowing, by rational means, the attributes that God possesses. This leads us to ask whether, not being able to know him rationally, it is no longer necessary to praise him. But if Hume considers that knowing is a simple recognition of existence without penetrating into the divine attributes, then worship does proceed.

[12] In general, the deism of the seventeenth and eighteenth centuries opts for the dissolution of divine revelations through the application of the rational criterion to them. For deists like Hume, religion and ethics must be considered natural facts; God the creator has no direct relation (at least not a cognizable relation) with the world which, once created, is governed by its own laws. Thus, prayer and theological hope lack meaning. Francisco Larroyo, in his introduction to the *Tratado de la naturaleza humana* (Mexico: Porrúa, 1992, XLVI), affirms that for orthodoxy and deism God is the first cause, transcendent, of all that exists. Moreover, God is a substance, something existing by itself. But

human reason lacks capacity to objectively demonstrate the existence of this first substance and universal transcendent cause. Substance and causality are nothing other than empirical forms of linking phenomena that repeat themselves and that, for this reason, provoke the acceptable belief that they will continue to present themselves. Outside of experience, substance and causality are fictions. With this, however, one does not intend to deny the existence of God. It is only indicated that it is not possible to prove it by rational means. Thus, agnosticism originates, the banner of positivist philosophy of the nineteenth century. [13] The third book of the *Treatise of Human Nature*, in its first part (of three that compose it), deals with morality in general (with virtue and vice). The central problem posed there is to demonstrate that moral distinctions (differentiating vice and virtue) do not derive from reason, and to this end Hume performs an analysis in which he concludes that virtue and vice are not objects of the understanding, basing himself on the study of relations of ideas or matters of fact (which are the two domains of knowledge). This analysis, however, is clarified in the *Enquiry Concerning the Principles of Morals*, so that the evolution of his thought becomes evident, not in terms of fundamental variation of content, but literarily, though this does not mean differences cease to exist, as we shall notice later with relation to the problem of the foundation of morality, where the change from an egoistic conception to a humanitarian and benevolent one becomes evident. Thus, for the presentation of his ethical theory we have based ourselves, fundamentally, on what Hume considered his most laudable work, the *Enquiry*, with the object of simplifying and making the contents more accessible.

[14] The nature of virtue and its definition is to be a quality of the mind that is agreeable or deserves the approbation of everyone who considers or contemplates it. In this way, vice is the action that is disagreeable and deserves censure.

[15] It should be clarified that, though there is no one for whom the appearance of happiness does not produce pleasure and that of misfortune unease, it is only the most generous souls who jealously seek the good of others and have a true passion for their well-being. With persons of petty spirit this sympathy does not go beyond being a light sensation that only serves to stimulate censure or complacency and that leads them to apply honorable or dishonorable appellatives to the object.

[16] Hume uses the concept of reason with diverse meanings, but we can consider it (unifying some of the most common senses that the author gives to the word) as the faculty charged with the discernment of truth and falsehood, which is exercised or operates either through abstract reasoning (relations of ideas) or through the probable (matters of fact).

[17] Eudemonism literally means possession of a good demon—that is, enjoyment or delight in a mode of being by which one attains prosperity and happiness. Philosophically, this concept is understood as any ethical tendency according to which happiness is the supreme good. For Hume that happiness is obtained in the search for the common good.

[18] For Hume, the distinctive impressions of moral good or evil consist only in a particular pain or pleasure.

[19] Let us understand by egoism the direction of conduct according to personal interests, based solely on pain or pleasure.

[20] Carlos Mellizo in the introduction to David Hume's work, *Historia natural de la religión*, p. XXI.

[21] That disturbance due to the fact that some human beings intend to obtain what others have worked for derives from egoism, fed by the few possessions they have in relation to their needs, and to restrict this egoism human beings must distinguish between their own goods and those of others. Justice takes its origin, then, from the egoism and limited generosity of human beings, together with the scarce provision of goods that nature grants for their needs.

[22] The promise arises in the following way: the advantage of mutual aid in society is obvious: someone helps another so that in turn the latter will help him when the former so requires. But one of the two might refuse to provide the aid, so a verbal formula of words

called "promise" is invented by which the person expresses the resolution to do something and exposes himself to being punished with distrust if he does not do it.

[23] These are the principles that currently govern the market or commerce: each one respects the goods of others, the transfer of goods, the fulfillment of established promises.

[24] Hume explains his proposal in detail, establishing the exact number of magistrates and senators, which, however, does not interest our purposes of expounding the most adequate system of government, since Hume's calculations are based exclusively on his country.

[25] The people govern by electing their representatives; *demos*, people; *cratos*, power.

[26] It should be clarified that Hume is one of the greatest pillars of modern philosophy, since, unlike antiquity which saw philosophy as the science of divine and human things and unlike the Middle Ages which saw it as the science of the transcendent, in Hume philosophy focuses solely on the human dimension.

[27] We have defined the good, in the chapter on ethics, as identical to the agreeable or pleasant, and evil, by necessary consequence, as the disagreeable.

ABOUT THE AUTHOR

Luis Arturo Pelayo Gutiérrez holds a bachelor's degree in philosophy and a master's degree in philosophy and cultural criticism from the Universidad Intercontinental (Mexico City), as well as a doctorate in philosophy from the Universidad Iberoamericana (Mexico City). He was a professor for more than a decade in the humanities area of the Instituto Tecnológico y de Estudios Superiores de Monterrey, at the Mexico City and Santa Fe campuses. In 2001 he obtained first place in the National Essay Contest on Values, organized by the Federation of Mexican Private Higher Education Institutions (FIMPES), and in 2016 received the Recognition for Academic Performance as professor of the Humanities Department of the Tecnológico de Monterrey, Santa Fe campus. Parallel to his academic activity, he developed his professional career in the editorial field at the Organisation for Economic Co-operation and Development, at the magazines *El Mundo del Abogado*, *El Mundo de la Educación*, and *Abogacía*, and was editor of philosophy works at the Fondo de Cultura Económica from 2003 to 2008, a publishing house where he received the Award for Effectiveness, Transparency and Innovation in 2006.

Thank you for investing your time in this book!

If it clarified Hume's philosophy for you,
I would be grateful if you shared a brief review
on Amazon.

Your feedback makes a real difference
for future readers.

If you'd like early access to my upcoming writings,
reflections, and exclusive content not shared publicly,
email luispelayo@hotmail.com with **Subscribe**
in the subject line.